PAPUA NEW GUINEA

Science

Grade 8

Teacher Resource Book

Kenneth Rouse

OXFORD

253 Normanby Road, South Melbourne, Victoria 3205, Australia

Oxford University Press is a department of the University of Oxford. It furthers the University's objective of excellence in research, scholarship, and education by publishing worldwide in

Oxford New York

Auckland Cape Town Dar es Salaam Hong Kong Karachi Kuala Lumpur Madrid Melbourne Mexico City Nairobi New Delhi Shanghai Taipei Toronto

With offices in

Argentina Austria Brazil Chile Czech Republic France Greece Guatemala Hungary Italy Japan Poland Portugal Singapore South Korea Switzerland Thailand Turkey Ukraine Vietnam

First published 2008
Reprinted 2009, 2013, 2014

Cataloguing-in-Publication data:

Kenneth Rouse

ISBN 978 0 19 555519 6

Typeset by Pier Vido
Illustrated by Uramina and Nelson Ltd
Printed in China by Golden Cup Printing Co. Ltd

Contents

Overview

Science

Science helps us to explore, understand and communicate information about the things that we find in the world. The scientific method provides students with a reliable way of finding out about the world and solving problems. The knowledge, skills and attitudes developed by science education will help students to prepare for playing a greater part in their community, and for further study or entry to the workforce. Science education helps students to make informed and responsible decisions about their way of life, their health, their environment and the kind of society in which they want to live.

Science for Grade 8 Student Book

Key features

The content of the student book is designed to be applicable to the wide range of learning contexts of students in Papua New Guinea. The success of implementing the science curriculum depends on the abilities of the teacher to adapt the curriculum and learning materials to the context of the local community. Consequently, the content is flexible in that students in both rural and urban areas can relate to the information. Both the text and the illustrations reflect diverse contexts such as islands, highlands and mainland coastal environments.

The content of this book supports student learning for the science curriculum area. The book:

- directly supports and supplements the upper primary syllabus by following the sequence of strands and sub-strands, with one chapter or section for each strand and clearly identifiable topics for each sub-strand
- contains direct references to the new upper primary syllabus at the beginning of each chapter, demonstrating the clear relationship between the student book and the syllabus
- provides topics and learning approaches that directly support the achievement of syllabus outcomes. The subject content is based on the topics listed under 'Recommended Knowledge' subheadings in the 'Elaborations' section of the *Science Teachers Guide*
- includes a wide range of student activities at the end of each topic (which can be completed inside and outside the classroom), reference information and a glossary of terms. Most activities in the 'For you to try' sections were derived from ideas under 'Recommended Skills and Suggested Activities' in the 'Elaborations' section of the *Science Teachers Guide*
- uses icons to indicate where book content has major links to other upper primary subjects and to indicate activities or investigations appropriate for assessment
- is written at a reading level that is appropriate for upper primary students and with a format that allows teachers to use it in ways that best suit their objectives and personal teaching style

- draws extensively on examples that are culturally appropriate to upper primary students in Papua New Guinea, giving recognition and credibility to Papua New Guinean knowledge and skills
- uses language that is gender-sensitive and includes positive gender roles
- uses text as the main medium of the activity-based approach and includes a good proportion of pictures and illustrations to support text
- requires only those **resources** that are normally available to teachers in Papua New Guinea, especially those in rural and remote areas
- includes summary questions at the end of each chapter.

Science for Grade 8 Teacher Resource Book

Key features

The Teacher Resource Book, in conjunction with the student book, will help teachers implement the science syllabus for upper primary students. It provides teachers with the following information:

- relevant information for planning a school-based program
- topics cross-referenced to other curriculum areas to allow for the development of integrated units of work
- a selection of teaching and learning strategies
- ideas for assessment activities
- topic elaborations to show how to develop topics covered in the student book into units of work
- how to extend and develop relevant content and contexts from the student book
- additional information that will assist teachers to develop their own units of work
- additional projects, investigations and activities to further extend students' skills.

How to use it

In order to make the best use of this book you will need to:

- get a sense of the information it contains and how it is organised
- become familiar with the strands and sub-strands, processes and skills, elaborations of learning outcomes, and teaching and learning strategies
- consider how to use the information to develop your own programs and units of work.

Structure

The Teacher Resource Book is structured in the following way.

- Each chapter covers one syllabus strand for science: (Strand 1: Working scientifically, Strand 2: Living things, Strand 3: Science in the home, Strand 4: Earth and beyond).
- At the beginning of each chapter there is an **overview page** which highlights:
  - ➢ the outcomes of the strand and sub-strands
  - ➢ how these outcomes are developed over the three upper primary grade levels
  - ➢ key words and concepts used and developed throughout the chapter
  - ➢ possible assessment tasks that could be carried out to assess students' knowledge and skills
  - ➢ identified content that has major links to other upper primary subjects.

- **Teacher information**—in this section, information is given which is additional to that already in the student book to enable teachers to develop units of work. A sample unit is also included in the Appendices to show how a unit of work can be developed over a period of time to achieve specific outcomes.
- **Equipment** needed for the investigations and activities—this section, with cross references to page numbers in the student book, lists what students will need in order to carry out the investigations, activities or projects in the chapter. Further notes on equipment are listed under 'Useful materials' on page 12.
- **Answers and explanations**—this section provides answers to some of the questions or includes suggested answers or an explanation or elaboration of the text of 'For you to try' questions.
- The **Appendices** at the end of this book include:
  - ➢ a sample unit of work
  - ➢ planning and assessment templates.

A **Glossary** is also provided.

- **Icons**—there are icons throughout the student book. The following icons indicate strong links to other subject areas. For example, when dealing with the strand **Science in the home**, there are links to the Personal Development strand: Our culture, values and lifestyle; and to the Social Science strand: Culture. The icons look like this:

ML = Making a Living

M = Mathematics

PD = Personal Development

L = Language

A = Arts

SS = Social Science

An **icon** is used to suggest which activities can be used for assessment: 

An icon is also used to remind students to write up a scientific report of an investigation using the headings Aim, Apparatus, Method, Results, Conclusion. This is explained further on page 13. 

Teaching and learning

Outcomes-based education

Outcomes-based education is used in many countries to identify and monitor progress in student learning. A set of outcomes is written to measure the success of teaching a learning unit, topic or course. These outcomes are measurable and can be used to assess if student learning has taken place. An outcomes approach to education means identifying what students should achieve and focusing on ensuring that they do achieve. It means shifting away from an emphasis on what is to be **taught** and how and when, to an emphasis on what is actually **learnt** by each student.

The impact of outcomes-based programs on teacher planning and assessment has been significant. Teachers have had to shift from focusing on teaching a subject to focusing on planning for student learning.

Learning outcomes

The science syllabus makes explicit the knowledge, skills, attitudes and values that students should achieve in Grades 6, 7 and 8 and these are expressed as learning outcomes and indicators. These outcomes describe specifically what students know and are able to do in each strand and grade. The outcomes are broad and can be achieved in any context depending on available resources and expertise. They are student-centred and written in terms that enable them to be demonstrated, assessed and measured.

A student-centred approach focuses on learning as being the active construction of meaning by students, and teaching as the act of guiding and facilitating learning. Examples would include:

- building on students' prior knowledge
- bringing the community and its resources into the school and providing opportunities for students to go out into the community to learn
- providing opportunities for problem-solving, decision-making and taking action
- providing students with opportunities to reflect upon their own learning, knowledge, values, attitudes and skills.

Learning outcomes are also developmental, showing progression from one level to the next. For example:

6.3.5 Identify and explain how simple machines can be used in homes and the community to do work.

↓

7.3.5 Identify and make recommendations on how simple machines can make life easier through community field study.

↓

8.3.5 Conduct investigations on simple machines and use problem-solving skills to establish the efficiency of the machine as a tool to do work.

Developmental outcomes aim to develop students who are able to:

- reflect and explore a variety of strategies to learn effectively
- participate as responsible citizens in the life of local and national communities
- be culturally sensitive across a range of social contexts
- explore education and career opportunities
- develop income-generating opportunities.

Each learning outcome is illustrated with a list of things that students know and can do in order to show that they are achieving an outcome. These are called *indicators*. Indicators are included in a syllabus to help exemplify the range of observable sample behaviours that contribute to the achievement of outcomes linked to the content. They can be used by teachers to monitor student progress within a level and to make judgments about the achievement of an outcome. It is important not to confuse indicators with content.

Learning outcomes and indicators will:

- give teachers the flexibility to develop programs to meet the needs of their students
- help teachers assess and report students' achievements in relation to the learning outcomes
- allow student achievement of the outcomes to be described in consistent ways
- help teachers monitor student learning
- help teachers plan their future teaching programs

- describe what most students will know and be able to do as a result of effective teaching and learning
- help teachers develop student activities for units of work.

In summary, outcomes provide a scope and sequence of student learning. They provide a useful focus for planning units of work and report student achievements. Indicators assist in the assessment and reporting process. Indicators assist in the achievement of learning objectives.

Strategies

The approach to science is student-centred and provides students with opportunities to practise critical and creative thinking, problem-solving and decision-making. It involves the use of skills and processes such as recall, application, analysis, synthesis, prediction and evaluation, all of which contribute to the development and enhancement of critical thinking. This approach also encourages students to reflect on and monitor their thinking as they make informed decisions and take appropriate actions.

While working towards their goals, students develop **communication** skills to enable them to work with others to discuss issues, needs, values, feelings, opinions and attitudes. These skills include:

- interpersonal skills of listening, speaking, responding, being assertive, questioning and justifying a position
- skills in presenting feelings, ideas, views, decisions and findings in written or graphic forms or through movement or drama
- literacy skills such as reading, writing and speaking in ways that suit the context and audience, using the specialised language of science.

The following three teaching and learning approaches and related teaching and learning strategies use a student-centred approach.

Approach 1: the 5Es

The 5Es approach is based on the idea that students learn best when they participate in activities that give them opportunities to work things out for themselves. There are five phases.

- Engage
- Explore
- Explain
- Elaborate
- Evaluate.

Approach 2: the interactive approach

The interactive approach involves a partnership in which student and teacher discuss and cooperate in selecting the topic in which the students are then active participants. There are five phases.

- Preparation
- Exploration
- Students' questions
- Investigations
- Reflection.

Approach 3: Predict, observe, explain

In this approach, students draw on their own experiences to make predictions. There are three phases.

- Predict
- Observe
- Explain.

More details of these approaches to student-centred learning are to be found in the *Science Teachers Guide* (pages 8–18).

Teaching methods

There are three main teaching strategies that can be applied for the learning of new information.

Theory learning (i.e. explicit teaching)—The teacher imparts knowledge or demonstrates skills. The teacher accordingly instructs students in what to do and how best to do it.

Practical learning—The teacher demonstrates the steps or processes of undertaking specific tasks. Students observe the demonstration, discuss processes and skills used by the teacher and then practise these skills and processes in a familiar setting.

Experiential learning—The teacher plans for learning to take place in the field or place of work. Here students gain new knowledge as they practise skills in real-life situations. This teaching approach stresses the active participation of students in meaningful activities.

Teachers need to use a range of teaching methods to ensure students not only gain the process skills but can also apply them to relevant real-life situations. Teaching methods to develop these process skills include the following:

Brainstorming—These are activities that are planned to stimulate discussion among students by sharing ideas and opinions on how best to investigate or how best to tackle specific activities and so on.

Surveys and questionnaires—These investigative activities generally go hand in hand with brainstorming. Students collect, collate and analyse **data** so that they can make informed decisions. A questionnaire is a specific written form where people can record written responses to surveys.

Demonstrations—These integrate sources of information to show specific steps in completing tasks. The teacher demonstrates a process and identifies what research and reporting skills (including the source of information) were used to complete the task.

Discussion/seminars—These teaching methods allow students to clarify thoughts and present information in a logical order within a formal format (seminar) or a less formal format (group discussion). Through exposure to these processes, students develop a deeper understanding of issues/problems and can present informed possible solutions.

Problem-solving—This is a specific process that students can apply to investigate a task for which there is no immediate or obvious solution and establish an action plan to come up with a possible solution. The major steps in problem-solving tasks are:

1. identifying the problem
2. selecting or developing a strategy to solve the problem
3. implementing the devised plan
4. monitoring and recording results
5. evaluating the results.

Presentations/reports—There are a variety of ways a teacher can organise presentations and reports. Reports may be part of a problem-solving task where students present their findings; this may be in oral or written form. They may be individual reports based on outcomes of specific investigative work (written or oral). Presentations by outside sources may be organised to present relevant information for students to use so that tasks can be completed, in particular, large tasks such as projects.

Cooperative group work—Many activities in everyday life require that people learn to work in groups. Through carefully monitored group work, students can experience working as a team. Teachers need to:

- organise their classroom layout in such a way that cooperative learning is encouraged
- plan activities that require students to work in pairs and small groups as well as individually

- construct activities where students consult each other, share ideas and learn from each other. The content to be shared should not be predetermined by the teacher.

Project work—This allows the teacher to create real-life situations where students develop their understanding and skills. They also develop communication skills as they need to talk to each other to reach an understanding. As a group, students have to use and apply basic research skills to locate relevant information as well as organised reporting skills to relay project outcomes. When devising projects teachers need to ensure that projects:

- use real-life or concrete examples
- encourage hands-on learning experiences
- are local and community-based
- provide purposeful and meaningful learning experiences
- promote critical thinking and problem-solving
- encourage interaction with a range of individuals and contexts
- encourage active community participation.

Planning

Planning, programming, assessing and reporting involve the consideration of the individual learning needs of all students and the creation of a learning environment that assists students to achieve the outcomes of the syllabus. Students' achievement of the syllabus outcomes is the goal of planning, programming and assessing. The sequence of learning experiences that teachers provide should build on what students already know and should be designed to ensure that they progress through the levels identified in the syllabus.

In an outcomes-based curriculum, lessons should be planned so that outcomes, assessment and classroom practice are all integrated. Assessment should not be tagged on to the end of a section of work but should be planned at the same time as planning the lesson content and should be ongoing.

Teaching programs need to be developed by teachers to structure learning experiences over a period of time. These programs should consist of:

A long-term plan—such as a yearly plan—where teachers identify and *develop* units of work that will be implemented over a long period of time. Teachers decide on the duration of these units of work in their long-term plan.

Short-term plans—These require the teacher to develop the units of work identified in the long-term plan. These units of work generally are planned to take 2–4 weeks.

Lesson plans—These are generally a further breakdown of the short-term plan (the type of lessons that will be undertaken to achieve the objectives of the short-term plan).

Planning guidelines

Teachers need to plan groups of lessons that enable students to achieve the outcomes described in the syllabus. You should fit each set of lessons into a short-term work plan. Use the following table as a checklist when planning lessons. Planning this way helps to align assessment with outcomes and with practicable teaching approaches in the classroom.

When planning, ask these focus questions.

- What do students need to know and what should they be able to do?
- What do they already know and what can they already do?
- How will I facilitate learning?
- How will I assess learning?

Lesson Planning Table

Outcomes	**Things to plan for**
1 Learning outcome or outcomes	Identify the outcome in the curriculum that you are working from.
2 Content: topic or key concept	To what theme do the lessons belong? (e.g. Simple machines in the community)
3 What will students learn in the particular lessons?	How will students achieve the learning outcome? List the appropriate • knowledge to acquire • skills to achieve • values and attitudes to adopt.
4 Number of lessons that need to be taught	How many lessons do you plan to teach on this particular topic?
Assessing progress	**Things to think through**
1 Evidence of learning	What will you look for in each student's work? Write down the knowledge and skills that are to be assessed (each one should be something a student can do).
2 The way learning will be assessed	Examples of methods you may use: • formal (oral or written presentation) • informal (teacher observation) • small task within a larger project • homework • test.
Classroom practice	**Things to consider**
1 Method or activity	What will you and what will students do and in what sequence?
2 Time	For how long will you explain or demonstrate new concepts? For how long will students do each activity?
3 Teaching methods	How exactly will you arrange students? • as a whole group • working in small groups or pairs • working individually. Where will students be? • in the classroom • outside.
4 Resources needed	List any resources you may need for students to complete tasks.

Assessment

Assessment should be an integral part of the teaching and learning process. Most teaching involves assessment, and by planning what to assess and recording the specific assessment information, appropriate assessment data can be collected.

There are a number of purposes for assessment:

- to collect and analyse information about students' learning
- to provide guidance, feedback and information about students achievements and progress to both students and parents
- to inform program decision-making and classroom organisational techniques.

The most important purpose of assessment is to improve student learning. Assessment stems naturally from the teaching/learning situation. Teachers in their interaction with students constantly assess:

- students' current understandings
- the nature of any misconceptions
- students' current needs.

Assessing and teaching cannot be separated, and assessment should inform teaching. Assessment is about finding out what students know and can do. The teacher constantly needs to ask these questions.

- What do I want to know?
- How will I find out?

This should be an ongoing process as:

- assessing students continuously enables teachers to monitor closely and understand their progress
- ongoing formal continuous assessment helps teachers diagnose problem areas in both learning and teaching, and allows teachers to change their teaching accordingly
- students receive helpful feedback after every assessment.

Process of assessment

1. Provide students with opportunities to demonstrate what they know and can do in terms of identified learning outcomes.
2. Gather and record evidence of students' demonstration of learning outcomes.
3. Make judgments about students' demonstration of learning outcomes.

Assessment methods

The purpose, principles, and processes of assessment are clearly described in the *Science Teachers Guide* on pages 19–29. Assessment strategies selected by the teacher should be appropriate to the situation and to the purpose of the assessment. Teachers have the opportunity to observe and record aspects of students' learning in a range of situations.

Group work—The teacher can determine the extent of student interaction and participation.

Listening—Listening to students respond to questions as well as other input, the teacher can collect many clues about students' current understanding and attitudes.

Interviewing students—Teachers can collect specific information about the way in which students think about certain situations.

Other assessment methods can include:

- observation
- consultation
- analysis of students' work (examination of detailed evidence in student responses)
- self and peer assessment.

Other sources of information for assessment purposes include the following:

- samples of students' work
- oral explanations or demonstrations to others
- questions posed by students
- practical tasks
- investigations and/or projects
- students' oral and written reports
- short quizzes
- pen and paper tests.

Reporting

Reporting is a way of communicating accurate information about students' demonstration of learning outcomes in a timely way. The purpose is to:

- acknowledge and support students' learning progress
- inform parents about the students' learning progress.

Reporting modes include:

- written reports
- student–teacher conferences
- parent interviews
- final performance or presentation
- portfolios.

Science without a laboratory

Science is a practical subject and students should do as much practical work as possible. The term **Investigation** has been used to describe practical work or experiments and this reflects the philosophy of students finding out things for themselves.

While doing practical work, students will learn useful manipulative skills which are relevant outside the science lesson and also learn to solve practical problems. Practical work also allows them to experience the process of science rather than learning only from books. More importantly, practical work is enjoyable and an effective way to learn.

Most primary schools do not have laboratories or special science equipment, but this should not discourage teachers from doing practical work with students. At the upper primary level, science can be taught by using resources that are locally available. These resources include those that are available in the natural environment, things which have been thrown away and can be recycled, and things which can be bought in local stores.

The investigations have been written in such a way that they require only those resources that are normally available to teachers in Papua New Guinea, especially those in rural and remote areas.

Teachers should try out the investigations before the students do them so that they understand the skills needed and the kind of problems that students are likely to face when doing them.

Useful materials

A lot of useful materials are thrown away and can be recycled. Teachers should always be looking for things which can be used to teach science. For example, carpenters and electricians usually leave a few nails or short pieces of wire on the ground where they have been working. Make a collection of these materials and keep them safely in a box so that you have them ready when you need them. You will also need to be innovative and creative to come up with solutions to particular problems.

The students should also be encouraged to think in this way and to collect the materials that they will need for their experiments or to put into the box for later use. Talk to the students at the beginning of the year and also remind them regularly so that they can look for and collect useful materials. Collecting materials in this way will increase their involvement and enthusiasm.

Some suggestions for useful materials to collect are given here.

Glass jars
Glass bottles—various sizes
Plastic bottles (easily cut with a knife or pair of scissors)
Plastic containers
Tins and tin lids
Aluminium drink cans (easily cut with a knife or pair of scissors)
Polystyrene and plastic meat trays
Polystyrene and plastic cups
'Tetrapak' containers—rectangular drink containers that come with their own plastic straw
Plastic knives, forks and spoons
Plastic bags
Wooden and plastic cotton reels
Rubber bands
Pieces of string
Small pieces of blackboard chalk
Short pieces of candle
Old newspapers
Cardboard tubes from inside toilet rolls
Plastic bags
Pieces of material or fabric
Paper clips
Nails
Metal washers
Corks from wine bottles
Pieces of wire—tie wire and electrical wire
Old bicycle and truck inner tubes
Short pieces of plastic or rubber water hose
Magnets—from the speaker of an old radio cassette player, an old computer, an old electric motor or from the rubber strip around the door of an old fridge or freezer
Lengths of bamboo tube or plastic waste pipe
Sand
Cement
Rocks
Fossils

Safety in science

Carrying out investigations in science can involve risks. The activities in the student book have been written with safety in mind and the investigations are safe when carried out sensibly, but there is some level of risk in everything we do. Teachers must take reasonable precautions and ensure that students do the same. Teachers have a duty of care to identify possible risks and take action to reduce the risks.

When students go outside to do investigations in the local area, teachers also need to consider the safety issues involved and remind the students of ways to stay safe. Reducing the risks will ensure the safety of all students and others who may be nearby. When teachers try out the investigation before the lesson, they should also be thinking about safety issues.

Rules for working safely in science

Some suggested rules for Grade 8 science are given below. You might like to make a similar list that is suitable for your students. You could make this into a poster to discuss with your students and display on the classroom wall.

Always work quietly and carefully and be careful of others when you move around the room or whenever you are doing an investigation.
Never run when carrying equipment or near people doing an investigation.
Always read and understand the steps in an investigation before you begin.
Always follow the instructions given by the teacher.
Never taste substances unless you know it is safe to do so.
Tell your teacher immediately if you have an accident.

Writing up experiments, investigations or practical reports

Scientists have special ways of answering questions and solving problems. Scientists also have a special way of writing about their experiments which is related to the scientific method and is called a **practical report** or **scientific report**.

A practical or scientific report gives a list of the equipment and other things that were used as well as step-by-step instructions so that other people can understand what the scientists did and can repeat the experiment for themselves if they want to. Because scientists all over the world use this method, they are able to understand and evaluate each other's work, and communicate with each other. Most reports use the following headings or something similar.

- **Aim:** states the problem, question or purpose of the experiment.
- **Apparatus:** lists the equipment used in the experiment.
- **Method:** instructions used to carry out the experiment. This sometimes includes diagrams.
- **Results:** the observations or measurements that were obtained. Results are sometimes given in tables or graphs. A discussion of the results may be included.
- **Conclusion:** the answer to the aim or problem being investigated.

Students were introduced to this way of writing up an experiment in **Strand 1: Working scientifically** in Grade 6. Students should be encouraged to use this approach when they carry out an investigation. The **icon** is used in the student book to remind students to use this method regularly. Teachers should continue to check the progress that students are making in this skill and give suggestions about the way that they can improve their writing up of investigations. Being able to write a clear step-by-step report that is easy to understand and shows you can organise ideas under different headings is an important skill in science, and in other subjects. It is just like telling a story with a beginning, middle and an end.

STRAND 1 Working scientifically

About this strand

This strand begins by looking at the importance of good observation skills in order to understand the world around us and be able to solve problems. The idea of being **fair** that was introduced in Grade 7 is further developed, especially the importance of designing investigations or experiments that have a **test** and a **control**. This is achieved by criticising experiments that students have designed and carried out and offering suggestions for improvement. Carrying out fair experiments that can be repeated and provide similar results and reliable information will also give us confidence in the results. This leads to the different ways that we can show the information or data that we collect, such as drawing tables and various types of graphs. Each type is introduced together with rules and notes to guide students in drawing them. Being able to draw tables and graphs will enable students to sort information into groups so that they can quickly see the information and look for patterns in the results.

The strand further develops by looking at the importance of science in the global environment, in particular the ways in which scientific methods can help us to understand the world and to improve life in the community. Students consider various applications of science and the strand concludes by looking at the ways in which we can use our knowledge of science to manage the environment, in particular managing forests and managing the seas in Papua New Guinea and elsewhere.

Sub-strand 1

Main ideas

Sub-strand 1: Identify the role of science in the global environment and apply scientific methods to create solutions to problems.

Key words

Fair, test, control, confidence, reliable, data, patterns, table, column graph, bar graph, line graph, global environment, application, management.

Key facts

- People want to understand the world around them and find out the answers to many different questions.
- A good way to find out more about why things happen and how they work is to carry out scientific investigations, which usually means that we try to find the answer to a question.

- When we carry out an investigation we must make sure that we are asking a question that will help us to understand and then choose a way to find an answer to that question.
- When we carry out investigations we must also try to make sure that we are being fair, and this usually means that we must use controls.
- Each investigation will be different because it has a different purpose, but we must always be accurate in the way we collect and record information.
- The conclusions that we make must be based on the information that we have collected and be linked to the purpose of the investigation.
- When we think that we have found an answer we must look at the question again and decide if the answer is sensible or reasonable.
- When we use the scientific method to collect reliable information and answer questions we can make good decisions about the way that we can use science in everyday life.

Assessment tasks

Assessment aims to gather information on how well students have achieved the outcomes of the strand. A variety of strategies should be used: written, oral and practical.

- Each assessment item should be based on criteria that have been clearly written down. Students should be told what the criteria are so that they know the basis for judgment of their achievement and demonstration of the outcomes.
- Assessment should also be continuous and collected throughout the learning process by the completion of appropriate activities such as those indicated with the assessment icon in the 'For you to try' sections.

Major links to other subjects

Strand 1: Working scientifically builds upon ideas introduced in Culture and Community at the elementary level and Environmental Studies at the lower primary level. At the upper primary level, **Working scientifically** links to the strand Health of Individuals and Population in Personal Development. Aspects of different subjects can be integrated into activities such as:

- a project to improve life in the community
- collecting and analysing statistical data for specific groups in the community
- designing posters or performing a drama to relay the message of the benefits of using the methods of science.

Links with other subjects are noted with an **icon** in the student books.

Teacher information

Teachers should further develop the ideas about working scientifically that were introduced in Grade 7. However, as previously emphasised at Grades 6 and 7, teachers should again remember that working scientifically is something that should be achieved throughout the Science course. While it is important to teach the concepts outlined in this chapter, working scientifically is not something that can be taught as a separate topic but should be integrated into every topic and activity.

Being observant

Observation is a key skill that is used in the scientific method and we can all train ourselves to be good observers by being interested in what is happening and paying careful attention. In order to be good at investigating and solving problems, we need to be observant and try to understand what is happening by thinking about the things that we observe. This means that we must notice the things around us and pay attention to the details.

Doing experiments and using controls

The important ideas that were introduced in Grade 7 are revised and extended. Being able to design and carry out a careful scientific experiment according to accepted guidelines is essential in all branches of science and is also very relevant and practical outside science. For example, research to test a new medicine or the use of a new treatment to make sick people healthy again uses the scientific method. Medical scientists use the same method of a test and a control, but instead of using the word 'test' they often use the word 'case', and so they do a case-control study. These experiments provide the evidence that doctors need in order to decide if a medicine or treatment is effective and will make a patient better.

Doing a fair experiment

This principle is again illustrated by looking at two imaginary experiments designed and carried out by students. Students must criticise these and provide suggestions as to how they could be improved. They then have the opportunity to design an experiment of their own and apply the principles.

Confidence in our results

Important ideas that are developed here are that experiments that are well designed are fair and able to be repeated, and provide similar results each time. When this happens the information is more likely to be reliable and believable so that we then have confidence in our results. However, when we think that we have found an answer we must still be ready to look at the question again and decide if the answer is sensible or reasonable. We must be ready to doubt the quality of the information and try to check it. This important point is illustrated with the example of an imaginary group of students providing information about the fastest runners in their school. Does it sound reasonable or not? A person with a questioning mind will realise that the information needs to be checked.

Again, this is an important skill that is highly relevant to everyday life. Being willing to question information that we hear, and look for evidence is more likely to prevent us being tricked or misled.

Showing data

Students will be familiar with the idea of collecting information but may not know the word **data**, which means the same. When we take measurements we end up with a list of numbers and this topic introduces students to the ways in which we can show information so that it is easy to see and understand. One of the key skills of a scientist is to be able to interpret the results and one way of doing this is to look for any patterns.

Drawing tables and graphs

The skills of making tables and drawing different kinds of graphs are described. Rules are provided to guide students in these skills and they may need help with such things as choosing a suitable scale. Teachers should provide opportunities for students to practise the skills of both drawing and interpreting graphs.

Science in the global environment

This topic is a very important conclusion to the strand. The earlier topics develop the idea that science can help us to find out about and understand the world. Students now learn more about the applications of science and the way that we use science knowledge and skills to make choices about the way that we live and when we need to understand information about our environment. This theme is developed by looking at the ways that we can use science to make decisions about how we manage the environment, in particular managing the forests and managing the seas. These two examples are chosen because of their particular relevance to Papua New Guinea, although both of these issues are very important to all countries and people since they affect everybody. A case study is included that looks at the Hunstein Wildlife Management Area in the East Sepik.

Equipment needed for the activities and investigations

To complete the investigations in this chapter each group of students will need the following.

For you to try (page 5)

4 Investigation: Which fruit is that?

- A piece of cloth for a blindfold, a pair of gloves and a variety of fruits that are in season such as banana, orange, lemon, lime, pomelo, breadfruit, custard apple, mango etc.

For you to try (page 9)

2 Investigation: To find the light conditions in which seedlings grow best

- Some seeds, plastic containers, water, shade house made from bush materials, ruler. Each group should try a different type of seed.

Answers and explanations

For you to try (page 5)

1 The tray on the left has a jug and five glasses, three of which have straws. The tray on the right has a serving dish with a lid, two mugs containing a hot drink and a third container (possibly another mug with a hot drink) and a tall container at the back.

2 If students turn the book on its side and look very carefully, they should be able to read: 'THE SECRET MESSAGE IS' and then turning the book the right way again, they should be able to read 'I LOVE YOU'.

3

Item	Sight	Hearing	Touch	Smell	Taste
bicycle	✓	✓	✓		
mustard leaf	✓		✓	✓	✓
rice	✓		✓		✓
aeroplane	✓	✓	possibly	possibly	
rock	✓		✓		
soup	✓			✓	✓
body spray	✓	✓	✓	✓	

4 Investigation: Which fruit is that?

- In this investigation students should realise that our senses are more effective when they are used together. Many students will find it difficult to guess the fruit they are tasting when they are blindfolded or cannot touch or smell the fruit.
- Our observation and understanding of something depends on the information that we receive from all our senses, although we do not always realise this, especially when all our senses are working properly. If one or more senses is not able to be used then we notice that information is missing. People with a disability such as loss of sight or hearing may receive less information through that sense, but making greater use of the other senses can sometimes help to overcome the disability.

5 **a** on the floor where it fell = 2
b on the floor where it was thrown = 3
c on the blackboard = 1.

6 A

7 Answers will vary but some possible qualities are shown in the table below. The importance of each quality is difficult to assess and depends on individual circumstances.

Qualities of a good investigator	Importance
Understand the causes of **pollution**	high
Understand the effects of pollution on plants and animals	high
Understand the effects of pollution on people	high
Know how to find information about similar cases of pollution	may be high in some cases
Understand how to design and conduct experiments on pollution like testing water and living things	may be high in some cases
Know how to collect evidence and make decisions without being afraid of other people (especially those who may be responsible for the pollution)	high
Be able to communicate with local people who may be affected by the pollution—to collect information from them and provide information to them	may be high in some cases
Know how to get local people to cooperate—for example, in collecting information about the pollution	may be high in some cases
Be able to communicate with public servants who may be involved in the case, e.g. from Department of Environment and Conservation	may be high in some cases
Be able to communicate with political leaders—local, provincial, national	may be high in some cases

For you to try (page 9)

1 Some notes to help Group A:

- In your experiment you gave the three pots different amounts of water and sunlight so you changed two things at the same time.
- This means you don't know if the amount of water or sunlight was the main reason why the plants were green and healthy.
- So you cannot make any definite conclusions because you don't know the reasons for the results.
- Your group concluded that seedlings from this plant grew best in full sunlight because they were green and healthy. But your conclusion does not follow from the method you used and the results that you got.
- You must change only one thing at a time. If you want to find out about the effect of water and sunlight then you need one experiment with a test and control changing the amount of water. Then you need another experiment with a test and control changing the amount of sunlight.
- Because you put many seeds in the same pot there may have been competition between the seedlings to get enough nutrients from the soil. It would be better to have more pots but put fewer seeds in each pot. This would reduce the competition, and if the seedlings in one pot die you may still have seedlings in the other pots.
- You did not measure the height of the seedlings but only looked at the appearance of the seedlings. Measuring the height of the seedlings would provide extra information that would tell you which seedlings are growing best.

2 Investigation: To find the light conditions in which seedlings grow best

- The results of this experiment are open-ended and will depend on the type of seeds that are chosen and the conditions in which they are grown.

For you to try (page 10)

1
- Perhaps the 100-metre track has not been measured out accurately—it is shorter than it should be so students seem to run faster times.
- The stopwatch that is being used might not be accurate.
- The student reading the stopwatch might not know how to use it properly.
- The results might have been written down or copied incorrectly.
- Somebody might be playing a practical joke.

Students could check their results by doing the following, or getting a different person to do it so that any errors are not repeated by the same person:

- Measure the distance again with a tape measure or trundle wheel that is known to be correct.
- Check that the stopwatch is accurate.
- Check that the times have been written down correctly or copied correctly.

On 9 September 2007, 24-year-old Asafa Powell from Jamaica set a new world record in the 100 metres, sprinting the distance in 9.74 seconds at a competition in Italy.

2 Answers will vary depending on the dates that the students choose, but some alternatives are given below. Unless there is a major change in Papua New Guinea, the population looks like it will continue to double every thirty years. The population could increase more slowly if large numbers of people die from disease or if people begin to have fewer children.

Population of PNG		
Year	**Population**	**Comments**
1975 (Independence)	3 000 000	an estimate, not based on a census
2000	5 190 786	results from the census—number of people counted
2005	5 887 000	an estimate—the population seems to have doubled in about 30 years
2030	10 381 572	based on doubling of the population counted in the 2000 census
2035	12 000 000	based on the doubling of the estimated population in 2005 and rounded up to the nearest million
2060	20 763 144	based on doubling of the population estimated in the 2030
2065	24 000 000	based on the doubling of the estimated population in 2035 and rounded up to the nearest million

For you to try (page 13)

1

Test score	Number of students		Test score	Number of students	
20	II	2	15	II	2
19	~~IIII~~	5	14	IIII	4
18	~~IIII~~ III	8	13	I	1
17	III	3	12	-	-
16	IIII	4	11	I	1

2 a 7
b 61–65 kg
c 41 kg
d 75 kg
e 30
f The age of the students and their sex.

For you to try (page 15)

1

Temperature in school grounds		
	Temperature	
Time	in Sun (°C)	in shade (°C)
8 am	19	18
9 am	21	20
10 am	23	22
11 am	26	23
12 noon	29	25
1 pm	31	26
2 pm	32	27
3 pm	30	26
4 pm	27	23
5 pm	25	21

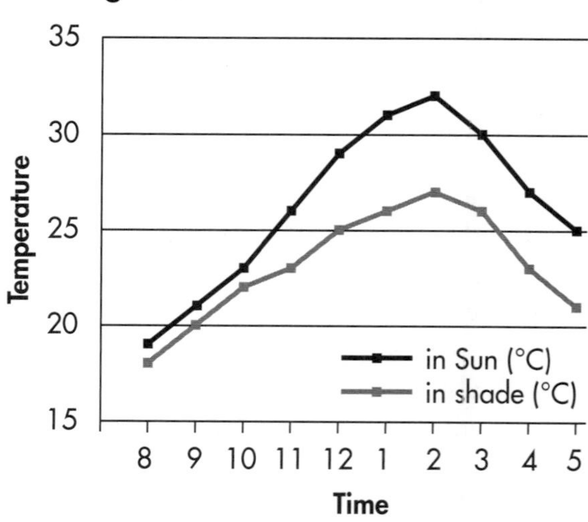

2

Comparison of water use in Port Moresby and Lae		
Water use	Percentage used in Port Moresby	Percentage used in Lae
Bathroom	16	22
Toilet	14	19
Laundry	10	13
Kitchen	5	4
Garden	55	42

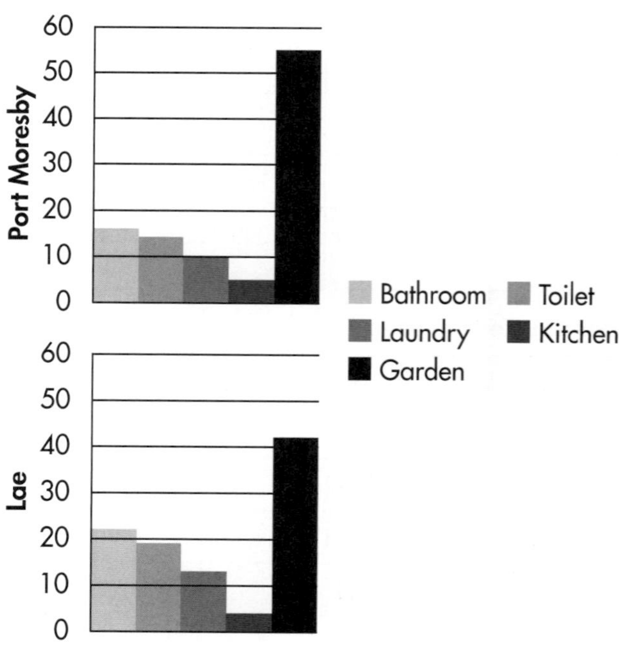

3

Number of wagtails seen on the 15th day of each month							
Month	**Wagtails**	**Month**	**Wagtails**	**Month**	**Wagtails**	**Month**	**Wagtails**
January	23	April	24	July	10	October	14
February	29	May	17	August	9	November	16
March	33	June	12	September	8	December	20

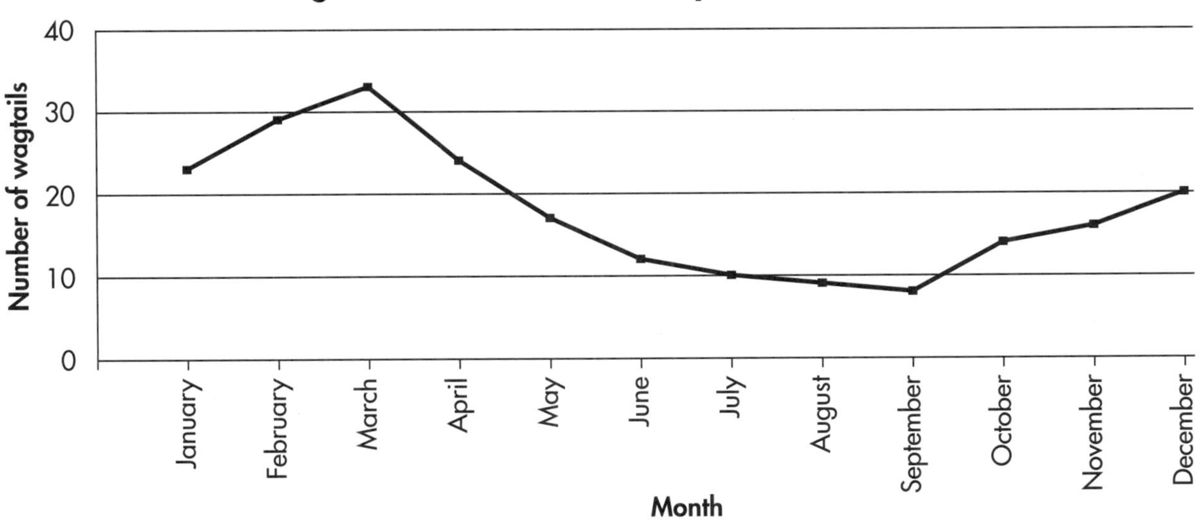

For you to try (page 20)

1 **Selective logging** means choosing the size of the trees that are cut down, for example, only cutting trees with a diameter between 50 centimetres and 150 centimetres. This allows the small trees to continue to grow under the bigger ones that are also left and so helps the forest to regenerate.

Clearfelling means cutting down all the trees in an area of the forest regardless of their size. Some logging companies do this.

2 Answers will vary but some advantages and disadvantages are given below:

Living in a Wildlife Management Area	
Advantages	**Disadvantages**
Able to continue to make sago	Lack of development e.g. roads, bridges
Able to continue to go hunting	Less opportunity to earn money
Able to continue to collect useful plants	Fewer people may want to live in the area
Able to continue to live a subsistence way of life	
Able to maintain traditional culture	
Able to continue with traditional economy	
Able to earn money from sustainable use of the forest e.g. portable sawmilling, butterfly and orchid farming	
Environment is not destroyed	
No pollution	

For you to try (page 25)

1 Methods of managing the seas are as follows:

- Control the number of fish that are caught. If too many fish, prawns or lobsters are caught by fishing then there will not be enough left to reproduce and the population will reduce so that there will not be enough to catch. This has already happened in some parts of the world.
- Control size of fish that are caught. When smaller, younger fish are caught, they are not able to reproduce and the adults in the population are not replaced. One way of doing this is to control the size of the nets that are used so that the smaller, younger fish are able to swim through.
- Control the season when fishing is allowed. Fishing should not be allowed when fish or prawns are breeding or migrating because this will stop the **life cycle** of the fish or prawns and fewer will be produced.
- Control the use of **drift nets**. Drift nets kill all kinds of fish, as well as dolphins, dugongs, turtles and even sea birds. Because they are so long, drift nets can lead to **overfishing** and the dead animals that are not wanted are just thrown back in to the sea.

2 Answers will vary but some ideas are given below:

- To protect the plants and animals that live in natural environments.
- So that we can continue to use forests and the sea.
- So that we can continue to get bush medicine.
- So that we can continue to enjoy forests and the sea.
- So that future generations will also have things they can use and enjoy.
- Because forests act like the lungs of the world by taking in carbon dioxide and giving out oxygen.
- Because forests help to hold water in the ground and release it slowly, forming creeks and rivers.
- Because the roots of trees help to hold the soil together preventing erosion.
- To prevent people who don't care about the environment from just making a profit.

Summary questions

1 **a** touch
b taste
c touch
d hearing
e smell

2

When an experiment is fair …	T or F?
somebody else should also be able to repeat the experiment and get similar results	T
getting different results when the experiment is repeated will help us to feel more confident about our conclusions	F
repeating the experiment can help to fully understand the reasons why something is happening	T
we will always see a pattern in the results	F

3 A

4 C

5

Statement	T or F?
Science can help us to understand the world and to improve life in the community.	T
People who learn science are less likely to understand what is going on in the world than those who do not learn science.	F
Our knowledge of science is useful when we make choices about the way that we live and need to understand information about the environment.	T
The applications of science are examples of the ways in which we make use of science in our everyday lives.	T

6 B
7 D
8 C
9 B
10 People want to understand the world around them and find out the answers to many different **questions**. A good way to find out more about why things happen and how they work is to carry out scientific **investigations**, which usually means that we try to find the answer to a question. When we carry out an investigation we must make sure that we are asking a question that will help us to **understand** and then choose a way to find an answer to that question. When we carry out investigations we must also try to make sure that we are being **fair**, and this usually means that we must use **controls**. Each investigation will be different because it has a different **purpose**, but we must always be **accurate** in the way we collect and record information. The conclusions that we make must be based on the **information** that we have collected and be linked to the purpose of the investigation. When we think that we have found an answer we must look at the question again and decide if the answer is **sensible** or reasonable. When we use the scientific **method** to collect reliable information and answer questions we can make good **decisions** about the way that we can use science in everyday life.

Living things

Living things

About this strand

This strand further develops the ideas introduced in Grade 7 on the nature of living things and the relationships between living things. It consists of two sub-strands. The first sub-strand **Nature of living things** begins by looking at the importance of reproduction as one of the characteristics of all living things during the adult stage of the life cycle. Students find out about the two main types of reproduction, asexual and sexual. **Asexual reproduction** is covered briefly and **sexual reproduction** is explored in more depth beginning with the **flowering plants**. In the animal kingdom, the main groups that are covered are the insects, fish, **amphibians**, reptiles, birds and mammals. In looking at the process of reproduction, a recurring theme is the way in which each group of living things is adapted to the environment.

The second sub-strand again looks at **Ecology, relationships and interactions** between organisms in the environment. In this sub-topic students will find out more about materials that are available for people to use and their impact on food webs and the environment. Students begin by looking at **natural materials** and **raw materials** that can be used to make **processed materials**, including **synthetic materials**. The properties of materials are investigated since these are the main reason why a material is chosen for a particular purpose. Students also learn to distinguish between **renewable** and **non-renewable** materials and those that are **biodegradable** and **non-biodegradable**. Since the type of materials that we use and the way that we use them can affect food webs and the environment, students look at ways of getting rid of waste materials in order to stay healthy and protect the environment. The strand concludes by looking at ways of conserving materials, various methods of recycling, chemical pesticides and chemical pollution.

Sub-strands 1 and 2

Main ideas

Sub-strand 1: All living things pass through a life cycle that consists of different stages. During the adult stage in the life cycle living things are ready to reproduce. Reproduction is needed for the species to survive but it is not necessary for every individual plant or animal to reproduce.

Sub-strand 2: There are various kinds of materials available for people to use, both natural and processed, each with their own properties. Materials can be renewable and non-renewable and they can also be biodegradable and non-biodegradable. The type of materials that we use and the way that we use them can affect food webs and the environment.

Key words

Reproduction, **spontaneous generation**, **pasteurisation**, adaptation, asexual, sexual, simple or **binary fission**, **vegetative reproduction**, **budding**, **regeneration**, vegetative reproduction, **fertilisation**, **zygote**, **embryo**, **foetus**, **stamen**, **anther**, **carpel**, ovary, **ovule**, **pollen**, **pollination**, seed, **fruit**, **dispersal**, life cycle, **larva**, **exoskeleton**, **moulting**, **metamorphosis**, **nymph**, adaptation, parental care, **spawning**, materials, natural, raw, processed, synthetic, properties, renewable, non-renewable, biodegradable, non-biodegradable, conserving, recycling, pesticides, pollution.

Key facts

- All living things pass through a life cycle that consists of different stages.
- At some stage in the life cycle living things are ready to reproduce.
- Reproduction is necessary for the species to survive, but an individual plant or animal does not need to reproduce in order to complete its own life cycle.
- Reproduction can be asexual or sexual.
- In asexual reproduction the new individual is produced from one parent only. There are different types of asexual reproduction.
- In sexual reproduction the new individual is produced from two parents.
- In sexual reproduction the male sex cell and the female sex cell join together during the process of fertilisation.
- Fertilisation that occurs outside the body of the female is called **external fertilisation** and fertilisation that occurs inside the body of the female is called **internal fertilisation**.
- Different living things reproduce in different ways depending on the environment in which they live.
- All living things will eventually die then rot or decay.
- Materials that will rot or decay naturally are called biodegradable materials.
- Materials that will not rot or decay naturally are called non-biodegradable materials.
- We need to use all materials wisely, and understand how to get rid of non-biodegradable materials that are no longer useful.

Assessment tasks

Assessment aims to gather information on how well students have achieved the outcomes of the strand. A variety of strategies should be used: practical, written and oral.

Each assessment item should be based on criteria that have been clearly written down. Students should be told what the criteria are so that they know the basis for judgment of their achievement and demonstration of the outcomes.

Assessment should also be continuous and collected throughout the learning process by the completion of appropriate activities such as those indicated with the assessment icon in the 'For you to try' sections.

Major links to other subjects

Strand 2: Living things builds on ideas introduced in Culture and Community at the elementary level and Environmental Studies at the lower primary level. At the upper primary level, **Living things** links to the strand Health of Individuals and Population in Personal Development. Aspects of different subjects can be integrated into activities such as:

- a project to improve life in the community
- collecting and analysing statistical data for specific groups in the community
- designing posters or performing a drama to relay the message of the benefits of using the methods of science.

Links with other subjects are noted with an **icon** in the student books.

Teacher information

Reproduction

The experiments of Francesco Redi and Louis Pasteur are important historical examples that have become part of the foundation for much of the later work of scientists on reproduction and micro-organisms. The experiment that Redi designed and conducted is significant because it was one of the first that used a test and a control. Redi concluded correctly that the maggots did not come from the decaying meat or from the air but must have come from the flies. However, it is interesting that he still thought that spontaneous generation occurred in some cases such as worms that live inside the gut of some animals. It is important to remember that in 1668 scientific knowledge was not well developed and what was known was not easily communicated among people so he was clearly very advanced for the time, even though his understanding was also partly wrong. However, this also shows the way we must be prepared to change the way that we think and the way that we explain things when new evidence becomes available.

The work of Pasteur was important in our understanding of micro-organisms such as bacteria and the application of this work and the work of other scientists that followed has become very important in the food-processing industry.

The need to reproduce

One of the interesting points to note is that although reproduction is a characteristic of all living things and is obviously needed for the species to survive as a whole, every individual does not have to produce offspring in order to ensure its own survival. Teachers might like to explore the idea of the success of a plant or animal, both as an individual and as a species.

Asexual reproduction

This topic is dealt with briefly. At the upper primary level it is difficult for students to be able to see how very small organisms reproduce, especially without being able to use microscopes. However, many students will be familiar with the regeneration of animals such as sea stars and with the ways that we use vegetative reproduction in subsistence agriculture.

Reproducing with flowers

The flowering plants or angiosperms are the most widespread group of land plants. Land plants have existed for about 425 million years. The earliest **fossil** of an angiosperm, or flowering plant, is dated to about 125 million years ago. The number of species of flowering plants is now estimated to be in the range of 250 000 to 400 000.

Pollination

As well as insects and the wind, pollination can also be carried out by vertebrates such as birds and bats, particularly, hummingbirds, sunbirds, spider hunters, honeyeaters and fruit bats. Plants adapted to this method often develop red petals to attract birds but do not usually develop a scent because few birds have a sense of smell.

Reproduction in insects

Reproduction in insects is very varied and complicated and has been kept simple to make it easier for students to understand.

Reproduction in vertebrates

When looking at mammals and at humans in particular, teachers could link this topic with strand 7.4 in Personal Development.

Throughout this sub-strand teachers should stress that it is the adaptations of plants and animals in the way that they reproduce which enable them to be successful in a range of environments.

Ecology, relationships and interactions

The main purpose of this sub-strand is to further develop the basic ideas in ecology that were introduced in Grade 7 about the way in which plants and animals interact in the environment. Humans have the greatest effect of all living things on the environment mainly because of the way that we use materials, which changes the environment.

Using materials

Key concepts that are introduced are:

- natural materials
- raw materials
- processed materials—which includes synthetic materials.

Properties of materials

The ideas in this topic were also introduced in Science in the home in Grade 7, sub-strand 7.3.1 Learning about substances.

Renewable and non-renewable materials

The idea of renewable and non-renewable materials may seem strange to many students. However, it is important to realise that there is a fixed amount of resources such as the rocks containing **minerals** from which we obtain **metals** and the crude oil from which we obtain petrol, kerosene and many other chemicals and synthetic materials such as plastic.

It is very expensive to look for resources such as oil and minerals and because of the practical problems of extracting and processing them, as well as the cost, it is not always possible to use what we find. For these reasons a mine is not always able to be built when minerals are found and mines also have a limited lifetime. For example, the Misima gold mine had a lifetime of only fifteen years. It began in 1989 and mining stopped in 2001 although gold was still processed until 2004.

One of the biggest problems that the world is facing is oil production. Oil has provided the **energy** for economic growth and development in the world for 150 years. However, oil is a non-renewable resource and there is a fixed amount. The rate of oil production, which means the extraction and refining, is about 84 million barrels per day. This production has grown in most years over the last century, but once we go through the halfway point of all reserves, production is likely to decline, and so we will have passed the peak. Some scientists now talk about 'peak oil' which means the highest global oil production or the halfway point in using the oil reserves that we have. Peak oil does not mean that we will run out of oil, but it means we will run out of cheap oil. The oil that has been extracted so far has been the most suitable oil and the easiest to reach, which has kept the cost down. Oil companies will be able to extract other oil but it will reach a point where it becomes too expensive and then production will stop. This will have a major effect on all people in the world and so we need to make alternative plans to overcome this.

Living things

Biodegradable and non-biodegradable materials

Biodegradability is an important idea in ecology and waste management. Organic materials that can be broken down by small living things like bacteria and **fungi** are said to be biodegradable. Some bacteria require oxygen and some do not.

The speed with which different materials will biodegrade depends on the nature of the material and the conditions. For example, woollen socks might take up to five years and leather shoes up to forty years.

Many products that are biodegradable in soil such as food wastes, paper and wood will not biodegrade when we bury them in a rubbish dump because the conditions of light, oxygen and humidity are not suitable for the bacteria to begin the decay process.

Materials that are not biodegradable will break down very slowly due to the action of sunlight, air and water. For example, things made from iron and steel that are left outside will rust and slowly disappear into the ground. An aluminium can may take up to 100 years and some plastics may take hundreds of years.

Getting rid of waste materials and staying healthy

The collection, transport, processing, recycling or disposal of waste materials that are produced by human activity is known as waste management. The purpose is usually to reduce the effect of waste on human health and so that the environment is not spoiled or made unattractive. In recent years there has also been a greater understanding of the effect of waste on plants and animals in the environment and also more effort to try to recover resources from waste materials.

Waste management can involve **solid**, **liquid** or gaseous substances with different methods and knowledge needed to deal with each.

Waste management practices are different for developed and developing countries, for urban and rural areas, and for residential, industrial, and commercial producers. Some waste materials may be dangerous and these are described as hazardous. Waste management for non-hazardous residential and institutional waste in towns and cities is usually the responsibility of local government authorities, while management for non-hazardous commercial and industrial waste is usually the responsibility of the people who make the waste.

Conservation

Conservation has a number of different meanings. People who believe in conservation are sometimes described as the 'conservation movement'. People in the conservation movement want to protect natural resources, including plant and animal species and their habitats, for the future.

When the conservation movement began the important issues included fisheries and wildlife management, water, soil conservation and sustainable forestry. More recently the movement has broadened from the earlier emphasis on the use of sustainable yield of natural resources and preservation of wilderness areas to include the preservation of biodiversity, which is the wide variety of living things that are found in an ecosystem.

Recycling

Recycling is the reprocessing of materials into new products. Recycling generally prevents the waste of useful materials, reduces the consumption of raw materials and reduces the amount of energy used, which also reduces greenhouse **gas** emissions.

While recycling is to be encouraged, the collection of scrap metal in Port Moresby has led to a result that is not so good. People steal the drain covers on the side of the road which means that cars or people can fall in the drain or the drain can become blocked with rubbish that is carried into the drain.

Chemical pollution

The example of disease caused by chemical pollution from Minamata Bay in Japan has become one of the most well-known in the world. Because of the nature of the case and the fact that it has gone on for so long, it has helped in our understanding of what happens and how such an issue can be handled.

In Papua New Guinea people are concerned about the chemical wastes in the **tailings** that mining companies release into the rivers.

Living things

Equipment needed for the activities and investigations

To complete the activities and investigations in this chapter each group of students will need the following.

For you to try (page 33)

1 Investigation: Looking at fern fronds

- A number of different **fern** fronds and a magnifying glass.

2 Investigation: Making a mushroom spore print

- A mushroom and a sheet of plain paper.

For you to try (page 38)

1 Investigation: Looking at flowers

- A large flower, a razor blade and a magnifying glass. Suitable flowers should be available in most places throughout the year, but if they are not then teachers may want to think about the time that they choose to teach this topic.

For you to try (page 40)

1 Investigation: Seed dispersal

- A variety of different seeds.

For you to try (page 43)

1 Investigation: Mosquito life cycle

- A few mosquito larvae, and a clear plastic or glass bottle or jar with a lid.

2 Investigation: Looking at cocoons

- Some different **cocoons** from bushes and walls around your school, clear plastic or glass bottles or jars, pieces of cloth or net and pieces of string.

For you to try (page 49)

1 Investigation: Life cycle of the frog

- Some fresh **frogspawn** and a container such as a large tin, dish or bowl.

2 Investigation: Life cycle of the gecko

- Some gecko eggs and a clear plastic bottle or container.

Projects

- Materials to make a pond such as clay to line the hole, plastic sheeting or an old bath or shower tray.
- Water plants and small fish or other aquatic animals to put in the pond.

For you to try (page 51)

1 Investigation: Sorting materials

- Various examples of materials such as flour, sugar, milk, wood, cotton, some wool, a nail, a stone, some clay, a marble, a pen top etc.

For you to try (page 54)

1 Investigation: Using the properties of materials

- Various materials that can be seen inside the classroom and access to an area outside the classroom so that students can observe materials there.

For you to try (page 57)

1 Investigation: biodegradable and non-biodegradable

- Various materials such as fruit, vegetables, flour, sugar, milk, wood, cotton, some wool, a nail, a stone, some clay, a marble, a pen top, a plastic bag etc.

For you to try (page 58)

1 Investigation: Recycling paper

- Different kinds of paper or carton, such as newspaper, butcher paper, brown paper, cardboard (about one square metre per group), an old dried milk tin and a piece of flywire (about 15 cm by 10 cm), a plastic bag, and a glass jar.

Project: Recycling (page 61)

Useful things that other people are throwing away that can be recycled such as bottles, cans, plastic containers.

Answers and explanations

For you to try (page 31)

1 The first piece of evidence that helped to show that the theory of spontaneous generation was not correct comes from an experiment carried out by the Italian Francesco Redi in 1668.

Redi set up three jars each containing some meat. Jar 1 was open to the air, Jar 2 was covered with gauze that allowed air inside and Jar 3 was covered with parchment that did not allow air inside.

After several days he noticed that maggots appeared on the meat in the open jar but did not appear on the meat in the other two jars even though the meat was rotten in all three jars. However, maggots did appear on top of the gauze in Jar 2 where the flies had landed. He concluded that the maggots did not come from the decaying meat or from the air but must have come from the flies.

The second piece of evidence comes from an experiment carried out by a French man named Louis Pasteur in 1878. He believed that germs are found on all the surfaces of all objects, in the air and in the water and that these germs cause things like food to go rotten. He showed that when these germs are killed by heating to 55°C food will no longer go rotten. In other words the germs did not appear without reason but were tiny living things that could be killed by heat.

2 Redi set up three jars each containing some meat. Jar 1 that was open to the air was the test. Jar 2 that was covered with gauze that allowed air inside and Jar 3 that was covered with parchment that did not allow air inside were both controls.

It was a carefully designed and fair experiment. The main thing that he changed was the contact of flies with the meat. The flies could reach the meat in Jar 1 but not in Jars 2 and 3. So the maggots appeared in the meat in this jar. However, by using gauze in Jar 2, which lets air go inside, he was able to show that the flies had tried to reach the meat because maggots appeared on the gauze but not in the meat. By using parchment in Jar 3 he was able to show that preventing air from going inside did not prevent the meat from going rotten and no maggots were found on the parchment because the flies did not try to reach this meat.

For you to try (page 33)

1 **Investigation: Looking at fern fronds**
Students should easily be able to see the rough structures that contain **spores** under fern fronds without a magnifying glass, although a magnifying glass helps to see the detail. Spores are produced in a sporangium (plural: sporangia) and found in a group called a sorus (plural: sori). Sori may be shaped like a circle or a line and may be arranged in rows.

2 **Investigation: Making a mushroom spore print**
This simple investigation should give a result overnight. When the mushroom is removed students should be able to see the colour of the spores on the paper. The spore print is characteristic and is used to identify mushrooms. When a glass slide is placed under part of the cap the spore print can be placed over either a light or dark background to help see the spores more easily, or the slide can be viewed under the microscope.

3 Spores are single cells produced by organisms such as fungi, **mosses**, ferns and **algae** that allow them to reproduce. Spores are usually produced in large numbers and are very light which helps them to be dispersed on air currents.

Spores will only grow new organisms when they find suitable conditions, so many spores are wasted. Producing thousands of spores rather than a few spores is a way of increasing the chances of survival of the fern.

4 **a** 8
b 64
c 512
d 262 144

The numbers quickly become very hard to calculate but the main point is for students to understand the very rapid multiplication of bacteria over a few hours. This is the reason why food and other materials can decay very quickly and why sickness caused by an infectious disease can also develop very rapidly.

For you to try (page 35)

1 Mammals produce only a few **eggs** because fertilisation is internal which increases the chances of fertilisation and so few eggs are wasted.

2 In human beings a zygote is a fertilised egg, an embryo is a zygote that is growing and developing by cell division up until the third month. From the third month onwards the baby continues to grow and develop and is called a foetus.

3 Fish and amphibians, including many frogs, use external fertilisation to reproduce. The eggs are laid in water and a male swimming by can release his **sperm** into the water which carries the sperm to the eggs.

Advantages

- Since external fertilisation occurs outside the body of the female, the male and female do not have to come so close together.
- No special behaviour such as courtship is needed. The female does not have to accept the male and males will not need to compete with each other for a female.
- If different males and females are in the same area then this may increase the chances that eggs are fertilised by different males which can lead to individuals with slightly different characteristics, some of which may be useful.

Disadvantages

- Fertilisation may be less likely since the sperm have further to travel and may not reach the egg but be carried away by water currents.
- Many eggs and sperm may be wasted.

Most reptiles, birds and mammals make use of internal fertilisation during reproduction.

Advantages

- Increases the chances of fertilisation because the sperm are deposited very close to the egg and so have a short distance to travel.
- Fewer eggs and sperm are wasted.

Disadvantages

- The male has to be accepted by the female. This may involve special courtship behaviour before mating can take place.
- Females may compete with each other and males may compete with each other in order to choose a mate. The competition may lead to fighting and some animals could be injured.

4 Reproduction is one of the characteristics of all living things which means that it is one of the qualities that we can use to tell living things apart from non-living things. Because all living things die they must reproduce in order to replace themselves, otherwise they would all disappear. However, it is not necessary for every individual plant or animal to reproduce in order to survive. An individual can still live successfully without producing any offspring of its own.

For you to try (page 38)

1 **Investigation: Looking at flowers**
Students will find it easier to do this investigation with a large flower. Different groups of students could try using different flowers and compare the results.

2 Pollination is the process in which pollen is carried from one flower to another, usually by wind, water or an animal.
Fertilisation is the process that occurs when a male sex cell joins with a female sex cell. Fertilisation occurs in both plants and animals.

3 Pollination can occur in two main ways. When **self-pollination** occurs pollen is carried from stamens to carpels on the same plant. When **cross-pollination** occurs pollen is carried from stamens to carpels on another plant of the same type.
When cross-pollination occurs it can happen in different ways. Insects can carry pollen on their bodies as they move from flower to flower. The insects are attracted by the flower's smell or bright colours. They look for the sugary nectar inside the flower. Insects that can pollinate different flowers are wasps, bees, ants, beetles, moths, butterflies and flies.
Wind can carry pollen from one plant to another. Flowers that are wind pollinated are not usually brightly coloured, but they have parts which hang out in the wind. Wind pollination occurs in grasses, conifers and many deciduous trees.

For you to try (page 40)

1 **Investigation: Seed dispersal**
Main types of wind dispersal:

- gliders—seeds with two wings that look like the wings of an aeroplane
- parachutes e.g. dandelion
- helicopters or whirlybirds—seeds with a wing at one end, like a propeller or fan blade
- flutterers or spinners—papery winged seeds e.g. jacaranda
- cottony seeds and fruits—seeds with a tuft of cottony hairs at one end.

2 The four main methods of seed dispersal are animals, wind, water and mechanical methods.

3 Seed dispersal is necessary in order to maintain or expand the distribution of a population of flowering plants. Dispersal involves movement so the plant can move away from the parent or move away from the existing population. Members of a population of flowering plants need the same resources in the ecosystem. Overcrowding may mean that all the plants cannot obtain enough resources to stay healthy. Dispersal reduces the competition for resources among the population and they all benefit.

4 The method of seed dispersal used by flowering plants is described as being an adaptation to the environment because different plants make use of different methods in different situations. For example:
- Plants that have hooks or **burrs** can only make use of this method because they live where there are animals that have fur in which the seeds can be caught.
- Plants that have seeds that are carried by parachutes have adapted by making their seeds light enough to be carried. Heavy seeds cannot be carried in this way.
- Plants that have seeds that are dispersed by water have adapted by making seeds that float and such plants must live close enough to the water so that the seeds can fall into the water.
- Plants that have seeds that disperse mechanically have adapted by producing seed cases that split and twist as they dry and have seeds that are small enough and light enough to be thrown a short distance as the seed case explodes.

Living things

5 Tomatoes and cucumbers can be classified as fruits because part of the ovary becomes juicy or fleshy to form a succulent or juicy fruit. This is a scientific method of classification based on the way the fruit develops.

In everyday life we normally classify something as a fruit and vegetable depending on whether it is sweet and the way that we eat it. For example, mangoes, pawpaws and watermelon are usually sweet when they are ripe. Tomatoes do not taste sweet and are normally eaten with other vegetables and savoury foods and so they are usually considered as a vegetable.

6 Papua New Guinea has **quarantine** rules about bringing seeds into the country in order to prevent plant (and animal) diseases being introduced which could cause plants to become sick. For example, a disease that affects a subsistence crop such as sweet potato or taro could have a major effect on the capacity of people to grow enough food. A disease that affects a cash crop such as coffee or cocoa could easily spread through the whole plantation and either reduce the crop or make it unfit to be harvested. All countries have these sorts of rules which are based on the lessons learned from problems that have occurred in the past.

For you to try (page 43)

1 **Investigation: Mosquito life cycle**

Different kinds of mosquitoes have different kinds of larvae or wrigglers that behave in different ways. Some hang just below the surface skin of the water and others sink and rest on the bottom. Depending on the age of the larvae when they are caught, they should hatch into adults in a few days.

The lid should be kept on the container or it should be covered with a piece of flywire or mosquito netting so that the adult mosquitoes cannot escape. Not all mosquitoes carry diseases but it is best to be cautious and not increase the risk of being bitten.

2 **Investigation: Looking at cocoons**

Results will vary depending on the cocoons that students are able to find in the local area.

3 A life cycle is the term used to describe the different stages that a plant or animal passes through from the beginning of its life to the end. The appearance of some plants and animals is quite different at different stages in the life cycle.

4 **i** Silverfish and springtails have a life cycle that is called a no-change cycle. The adults lay eggs that hatch into young called larvae that look like the adult. Each larva grows until it is too big for its outside covering or exoskeleton. It then moults and loses the exoskeleton.

ii Grasshoppers, cockroaches, earwigs, termites, dragonflies, praying mantis, crickets and true bugs have a part-change cycle. This life cycle is also called incomplete metamorphosis and has three stages. The egg hatches into a larva which is called a nymph and looks very much like the adult. The nymph then slowly changes as it grows and wings develop from wing buds. It moults several times to become an adult.

iii Butterflies, moths, bees, wasps, flies, mosquitoes and beetles have a complete-change cycle. This life cycle is also called complete metamorphosis and has four stages. The egg is laid usually on one type of plant. The egg hatches into a small caterpillar or larva which spends most of its time feeding. It grows steadily and moults each time it becomes too big for its exoskeleton. At the end of the larval stage many insects spin a special case called a cocoon and fix themselves to a twig. The third stage of the life cycle is the **pupa**, which does not feed at all. Inside the pupa many changes take place as the larva develops into an adult. For example, wings, a mouth tube, eyes, legs, and many other parts develop. When the case splits open the adult or **imago** comes out which feeds until it is ready to reproduce.

For you to try (page 49)

1 **Investigation: Life cycle of the frog**
Students should be able to see the frogspawn hatch into **tadpoles** and then develop into young frogs.

2 **Investigation: Life cycle of the gecko**
Students should be able to see tiny geckoes hatch from the hardshelled eggs.

3 In frogs the female lays eggs in water or in damp moss or leaf litter. The male squirts his sperm into the water or the damp moss or leaf litter. The sperm are then carried to the egg by water and so fertilisation occurs outside the body of the female.

In lizards the male and female must come close together in order to reproduce. The male and female both have a small body opening called cloaca. The male holds the female so that the cloaca are close together. The male then passes sperm into the body of the female and fertilisation occurs inside the body of the female.

4 Since fertilisation in fish is external then development is also external and the eggs hatch into young fish outside the body of the female which is known as external development. Fertilisation is internal in pigs and so development continues inside the body of the female which is known as internal development.

5 Mammals such as the platypus and echidna are known as monotremes and lay eggs that have shells. The young develop inside the shell and then hatch as young adults.

Mammals such as the wallaby and bandicoot are known as marsupials and have young that are born prematurely. The embryo is very small and not well developed when it is born so it moves to the pouch of the female where it feeds on milk and keeps warm as it grows and develops.

Cats, dogs, pigs and humans are known as placental mammals and have young that complete their development inside the female. The embryo is joined to the mother by the placenta which provides food and oxygen and also gets rid of waste. Placental mammals are relatively well developed when they are born and look like miniature adults but still need parental care as they continue to develop.

6 Vertebrates that produce large numbers of young are generally less well developed when they are born and do not take a lot of care of their young when they are born. Vertebrates that produce fewer young are generally more developed when they are born and show more parental care after the young are born.

For you to try (page 51)

1 Investigation: Sorting materials

Example	Main material	Natural / processed	Description
Flour	wheat	processed	fine white powder, made from wheat
Sugar	sugar	processed	white crystals made from the juice of sugar cane that has been heated and evaporated
Milk	milk	processed	white powder made from milk that has been dried
Wood	wood	natural	the trunk or branch of tree with grey bark
Wool	wool	processed	cream coloured fibres twisted together, made from the coat of a sheep
Nail	steel	processed	silver colour, sharp at one end and a flat head at the other
Stone	rock	natural	round and grey in colour, about the same size as a mango
Clay	soil	natural	dark brown soil with small particles and can be made into pots
A marble	glass	processed	clear glass ball with a coloured centre
Pen top	plastic	processed	blue hollow tube made to fit the top of pen

For you to try (page 54)

1 Investigation: Using the properties of materials

Answers will vary but some examples are given below:

Materials inside the classroom			
Example	**Main material**	**What is it used for?**	**Properties**
Roof	iron with a coating of zinc	keeping out the rain and the sun	**waterproof**, strong, **durable**
Floor	concrete	flooring	strong, waterproof, durable, flat, easy to sweep
Louvre	glass	letting in light, keeping out wind, rain and people.	**transparent**
Post	steel	holding up the building	strong, rigid, durable
Chalkboard	sheet of masonite	for the teacher to write on and students to read	flat, smooth, dark in colour, can be marked with chalk and cleaned
Electrical wires	copper covered with plastic	carrying electricity to the lights	good **conductor**, **flexible**
Tap on water tank	brass	getting water out of the tank	strong, metallic, able to be made into a simple machine
Umbrella	metal frame, plastic handle and fabric cover	staying dry when it rains	light, strong, flexible, waterproof
Ball	rubber	Playing games and sport	Elastic, light, can hold air inside
Rubbish drum	steel	Collecting rubbish	Space inside, strong, durable
Firewood	wood	Cooking food	**Flammable**

For you to try (page 56)

1 Answers will vary but some examples are given below:

Materials used	Biodegradable	Non-biodegradable
Towel	✓	
Exercise book	✓	
Thongs		✓
Plate		✓
Food	✓	
Kerosene lamp		✓
Water		✓
Soap	✓	
Pen		✓
Bedsheet	✓	

2 Answers will vary but some examples are given below:

Material being used	Natural or processed	Waste produced during use	Waste left at the end
Firewood	natural	smoke, carbon dioxide	ash
Battery or dry cell	processed	none	metal case with chemicals inside
Tin of fish	processed	none	empty metal can
Food	natural	none	faeces
Water	natural	none	urine
Petrol or diesel fuel in an engine	processed	carbon dioxide, sometimes smoke	particles may be left in the air
Drink in a plastic bottle	processed	none	plastic bottle

For you to try (page 57)

1 **Investigation: biodegradable and non-biodegradable**

Students should plan their own experiments but simply leaving each material out where it is exposed to the air, light and humidity at room **temperature** will mean that it is also exposed to microbes such as bacteria. There is not really a lot of planning to do but students should understand the conditions that are suitable for decomposition to take place such as temperature, humidity and being exposed to the air and light. However, some students may wish to discuss whether the materials should be covered or uncovered. Materials that are uncovered may also attract insects such as fruit flies and house flies that may also affect the process of decomposition.

Some biodegradable materials will start to rot quickly and students will use their sense of sight and smell to detect this decomposition. Students may need to decide when to throw away the rotting materials, especially if the smell becomes too unpleasant. Some materials will take much longer to decompose or may not decompose at all, so the experiment will need to run for long enough to obtain a result. The investigation could be written up in two parts to allow for this.

Another long-term investigation is to leave a plastic bag outside in the sun for many months in a place where it will not be disturbed or blown away. The plastic bag will break down very slowly due to the action of sunlight, air and humidity.

For you to try (page 58)

1 **Investigation: recycling paper**

Soaking the paper or carton overnight will help the students to do this investigation more easily because it takes time for the fibres in the original paper to break up. Metallic flywire will work best because it is stiffer but plastic flywire or even a piece of old mosquito netting on a simple frame could also be used. Students should be able to get satisfactory results although the quality of the recycled paper will be rough compared to commercially produced paper. However, the method described here is similar to that used to make recycled paper on a commercial basis.

2 The questions in a survey must be written with the objectives of the survey and the characteristics of the community clearly in mind.

Questions that are used in a survey or questionnaire are generally of two types:

- **Open-ended** questions that give the person much freedom in the way that they answer the question. These questions are usually easier to write but harder to analyse because the wide range of responses can make it difficult to collate the information and make generalisations. When we interview a person we usually use open-ended questions.
- **Multiple-choice** or **fixed-response** questions that have more structure and guide the person to answer in particular ways by ticking various boxes. These are harder to write but it is easier to analyse the responses because you can get numbers and percentages of people who respond in a particular way and can then make generalisations that can lead to recommendations.

  Examples of multiple-choice or fixed-response questions:

  Q Which of the following materials do you use at your home, outside or in your garden? (You can tick more than one box.)

Tin cans such as tinned fish or tinned meat	
Aluminium cans such as fizzy drinks	
Plastic bottles and other containers	
Plastic shopping bags	
Glass bottles	
Newspaper or other paper	
Dry cells or batteries	
Chemicals such as pesticides or herbicides	
Other—please specify	

Q For the materials that you use, how do you usually get rid of the waste materials that are produced?

Waste material	Throw in bush	Throw in sea	Burn	Bury in special place	Other (please specify)
Tin cans e.g. fish, meat					
Aluminium cans e.g. drinks					
Plastic bottles					
Plastic shopping bags					
Glass bottles					
Newspaper or other paper					
Dry cells or batteries					
Chemicals such as pesticides or herbicides					
Other—please specify					

Examples of open-ended questions:

Q Thinking about the materials that you use inside or outside your home, what can you tell me about any problems that you have to get rid of the waste that is produced?

Q Thinking about the waste materials in your community, what can you tell me about the way that people get rid of their waste?

Q If you are not satisfied with the way that people get rid of waste materials, what do you think should be done to make it better?

Many surveys combine both types of questions, often with multiple-choice questions first and then some open-ended questions at the end.

Keep the survey as short as possible. Do not ask questions if you are not going to use the information. For example, if you are interested in differences in the behaviour and attitudes of men and women and people of different ages then you need to record their sex and age, but if you are not interested in these differences then it is a waste of time asking their age and recording their sex.

Students and teachers will also need to think about the following:

- How will you obtain permission and agreement from people to take part in the survey?
- How many people will take part in the survey?
- How will the survey be given—will the person fill in their own survey or will the student ask the question and then fill it in for them?
- What will you do if the person does not understand the question?
- When will the survey take place?
- How will you collate the results and make general conclusions?

For you to try (page 61)

1 Poisonous waste materials carried in rivers will eventually end up in the sea. Very small amounts of the poison may be taken in by the first organism in a food chain, such as plankton. This may not harm the plankton but the poison can be passed to the next organism in the food chain. The poison is not excreted but slowly builds up inside the animal each time the animal eats. This can happen at each stage of the food chain and so it is called biomagnification. Many shellfish are filter feeders that stay in one place which means that biomagnification of poisons can happen more readily. People who eat fish and shellfish from the sea become part of the food chain and so may eat the poisons that have slowly built up in the animals they eat.

Projects

The useful things that are able to be recycled will depend on what is available in the local area and the opportunity to make use of them. Possibilities include glass bottles, aluminium cans, tyres and inner tubes, plastic containers and plastic bags.

Summary questions

1

Statement	True or false?
Reproduction is one of the characteristics of living things.	T
All living things eventually die so reproduction is needed for the species to survive.	T
Every individual plant or animal needs to reproduce in order to survive.	F
Different species reproduce in different ways, depending on the environment in which they live.	T

2 D

3 C

4 **A** – V
B – VI
C – II
D – III
E – I
F – IV

5

Statement	True or false?
Plants usually scatter their seeds close to the parent for protection.	F
Dispersal of seeds reduces the competition for water, sunlight and minerals.	T
Seeds that are eaten by animals must be digested before they pass out with the droppings and start to grow.	F
Seeds that are carried on the fur of animals usually have hooks or burrs.	T
Seeds that are dispersed by water always sink.	F
Mechanical dispersal is more likely to happen on a hot, dry day than on a cool, wet day.	T
Seeds that are dispersed by wind usually have wings or parachutes.	T

6 A

7 D

8

Statement	True or false?
All natural materials are renewable materials.	F
Materials that are renewable usually come from things that grow	T
Non-renewable materials usually come from non-living things.	T
Things that are biodegradable usually last longer than non-biodegradable materials.	F
Things that are biodegradable are usually made from renewable materials.	T
All synthetic materials are processed materials.	T
All processed materials are synthetic materials.	F

9 All living things pass through a life **cycle** which consists of different stages.

At some stage in the life cycle living things are ready to **reproduce**. Reproduction is necessary for the species to **survive**, but an individual plant or animal does not need to reproduce in order to complete its own life cycle. Reproduction can be asexual or **sexual**. In asexual reproduction the new individual is produced from one **parent** only. There are different types of asexual **reproduction**. In sexual reproduction the new **individual** is produced from two parents. During sexual reproduction the male sex cell and the female sex cell join together during the process of **fertilisation**. Fertilisation that occurs outside the body of the female is called **external** fertilisation and fertilisation that occurs inside the body of the female is called **internal** fertilisation. Different living things reproduce in different ways depending on the **environment** in which they live.

All living things will eventually die then **rot** or decay. Materials that will rot or decay naturally are called **biodegradable** materials. Materials that will not rot or decay naturally are called **non-biodegradable** materials. We need to use all materials **wisely**, and understand how to get rid of non-biodegradable materials that are no longer useful.

Science in the home

About this strand

This strand builds on the ideas that were introduced in Grade 7 about the situations in which science is found and used in everyday life. It consists of two sub-strands. The first sub-strand **Learning about substances** is mainly concerned with the properties of materials. Firstly students find out about the **physical properties** of materials or the characteristics of materials and how they behave. This then leads to **chemical properties** and the three important families of chemical compounds—**acids**, **bases** and salts. The sub-strand further develops by looking at the use of **indicators**—dyes that change colour when they are mixed with an acid or a base. Students then find out about the **pH scale**, which enables us to measure the strength of acids and bases. The sub-strand concludes by looking at **neutralisation**, chemical reactions in which an acid reacts with a base to form a salt plus water.

In the second sub-strand **Using energy in the home** students begin by looking at heat energy in greater detail. The relationship between heat and temperature is explained and this leads to the uses of heat and problems caused by heat. The movement of heat is described in solids, liquids and gases through **conduction**, **convection** and **radiation**. Students also find out about the ways in which we make use of our knowledge of conduction, convection and radiation in applications such as the **vacuum flask** and the **expansion** of metals.

Electricity is the second form of energy that is studied. Students find out about different kinds of **circuits** and the uses of electricity that depend on the three effects—the heating effect, the lighting effect and the magnetic effect. One of the most important uses of electricity is in electric motors which combine electricity and magnetism to produce movement. This topic concludes by describing ways in which electricity can be produced by reversing the effects that were described earlier.

The last topic in this sub-strand covers **force**, work and energy in more detail and introduces students to measuring force, measuring work and measuring energy. Students find out how to calculate the **mechanical advantage** and **efficiency** of simple machines.

Sub-strands 1 and 2

Main ideas

Sub-strand 1: Materials have different physical and chemical properties that can be useful and affect the choice of materials that we use. Acids and bases that occur in nature or that are made can be used by people in various ways.

Sub-strand 2: Heat energy and electricity are often used in the home especially for heating and lighting, although the electric motor also makes use of the magnetic effect of an electric current. Simple machines can help people to do work because there is a mechanical advantage.

Key words

Properties, physical, chemical, strong, **brittle**, malleable, ductile, transparent, **translucent**, opaque, conductor, **insulator**, **density**, **atmospheric pressure**, acid, base, salt, **alkali**, **corrosive**, indicator, **litmus**, pH, neutralisation, heat, temperature, thermometer, Celsius, conduction, convection, radiation, electromagnetic, vacuum flask, expansion, **contraction**, **thermostat**, appliance, terminal, circuit, circuit diagram, conductor, insulator, series, parallel, effect, **electrode**, resistance, element, **filament**, fluorescent, **armature**, **commutator**, lead accumulator, newtons, force-meter, spring balance, **joules**, **kilojoules**, **megajoules**, mechanical advantage, efficiency.

Key facts

- The materials that we use every day have different physical properties such as hardness, strength, density.
- When we use materials we choose those that have the most suitable properties. For example, some things will float and some things will sink.
- Some substances have different chemical properties. For example, some things are acids and some things are bases.
- Acidic and basic substances can be found in nature and are used by people in different ways.
- Acids and bases can also be made and used in everyday life.
- When we use energy in the home we often use heat energy and electrical energy.
- Heat is a form of energy that can make substances hot and can be controlled.
- Temperature is a measure of how hot a substance is.
- Electricity has three main uses or effects—heating, lighting and magnetism.
- Electricity must flow around a path called a circuit which we can draw as a diagram.
- Simple machines can help people to do work because there is a mechanical advantage.
- We can calculate the amount of work that we do and the mechanical advantage of different machines.

Assessment tasks

Assessment aims to gather information on how well students have achieved the outcomes of the strand **Science in the home**. A variety of strategies should be used: written, oral and practical.

Each assessment item should be based on criteria that have been clearly written down. Students should be told what the criteria are so that they know the basis for judgment of their achievement and demonstration of the outcomes.

Assessment should also be continuous and collected throughout the learning process by the completion of appropriate activities such as those indicated with the assessment icon in the 'For you to try' sections.

Major links to other subjects

Strand 3: Science in the home builds upon ideas introduced in Culture and Community at the elementary level and Environmental Studies at the lower primary level. At the upper primary level, **Science in the home** links to the strand Health of Individuals and Population in Personal Development. Aspects of different subjects can be integrated into activities such as:

- a project to improve life in the community
- collecting and analysing survey data for specific groups in the community
- designing posters or performing a drama to relay the message of the benefits of using the methods of science.

Links with other subjects are noted with an **icon** in the student books.

Teacher information

Learning about substances

The approach in this topic is to deal with physical properties first and then chemical properties.

Properties of materials

In this topic students are introduced to the concept of physical properties of **matter** in each of the three **states**. Atmospheric pressure is included as an example of one of the physical properties of air, and density is also described. Density is a difficult concept and the explanation is kept simple, avoiding the use of units.

Investigating acids and bases

Most primary schools will not have the common laboratory acids such as hydrochloric acid, sulphuric acid and nitric acid or laboratory bases such as sodium hydroxide, ammonium hydroxide and calcium hydroxide. However, teachers can still achieve the outcomes of this unit using locally available materials.

Urine is also a weak acid that we all experience every day. Because urine is normally slightly acidic it helps to kill germs and protect against infection of the urinary tract. However, when a woman is pregnant her urine becomes slightly basic and she is more likely to have an infection of the urinary tract. A small amount of dilute urine could be tested with the red hibiscus indicator in the **Investigation: Making and using an indicator** on page 74.

The pH scale

This scale is included here so that students can understand that there is a way of measuring the strength of an acid or base. The strength of an acid or base depends on charged particles called ions and pH is a measure of the hydrogen ion concentration. It is also a special kind of scale called a logarithmic scale but upper primary students do not need to know about these details.

Neutralisation

Chewing betel nut with lime is also an example of a neutralisation reaction. Betel nut is acidic and without lime it tastes sharp or astringent and draws moisture out of the mouth. Lime is a base that neutralises the acid and helps to remove the sharp taste.

Using energy in the home

The first six indicators in **8.3.3 Investigate how energy changes from one form to another** are covered under the heading Using energy in the home.

Note that the last indicator in 8.3.3 is also repeated in 8.3.5. It is:

- *conduct investigations on simple machines to establish the efficiency of the machine as a tool to do work*

This indicator has been covered in **8.3.5 Conduct investigations on simple machines and use problem-solving skills to establish the efficiency of the machine as a tool to do work.**

The vacuum flask

Many modern vacuum flasks are now made of stainless steel instead of silvered glass. Stainless steel is a better conductor than glass which is a disadvantage in this situation although this kind of vacuum flask will still keep things hot or cold very effectively. However, the main advantage of stainless steel is that it will not break. The glass inside a vacuum flask is brittle and can easily break when dropped.

Expansion

Expansion can also be used to remove the metal cap from a glass jar that is hard to undo. Holding the jar upside down with the lid in hot water will make the lid expand a little so that it can be removed more easily.

Railway lines are another example of the problems caused by the expansion of a metal. In very hot weather the steel rails expand and may buckle. Special gaps are left between the lengths of rail to allow for expansion, but these gaps make the ride less smooth and also make the characteristic noise of a train running on rails. In order to help solve this problem a steel **alloy** has been developed that expands very little when it gets hot. When this steel is used to make rails, they can be welded into long lengths that give a much smoother and quieter ride. This is also known as continuously welded rail.

Electricity

The approach in this topic is to introduce some of the basic ideas such as conductors, insulators and circuits and then explain the three main effects of electricity—the heating effect, lighting effect and magnetic effect. The three effects are then used to help explain the main ways that electricity can be produced.

Force, work and energy

The earlier work in Grade 6 and 7 is extended here and calculations are introduced for the first time, which some students may find difficult. This is the most mathematical part of the Grade 8 Science syllabus and teachers may want to link this topic with other work in mathematics.

Measuring force

The force-meter or spring balance is the instrument used to measure force and students are able to make their own using locally available materials. Batteries or D cells are used to calibrate the force-meter because each D cell always weighs very close to 100 g and they are available everywhere. Remember 100 g is the same as one newton.

The force-meter will not be particularly accurate but will be perfectly adequate when used carefully and students should be able to understand the concept quite clearly. If you have a commercially produced spring balance you can weigh a number of D cells to check the **calibration** of the student force-meter. You can also compare the readings on the spring balance with the ones the students obtain on their force-meter and discuss any differences.

Measuring work

Students should understand that work cannot be measured directly using an instrument. Work can only be calculated by multiplying the force measured in newtons by the distance measured in metres.

Equipment needed for the activities and investigations

To complete the activities and investigations in this chapter each group of students will need the following.

For you to try (page 67)

1 Investigation: Properties of matter

- A selection of different materials to test: a rubber band, a piece of chalk, a stone, a glass marble, an aluminium can, a nail, a piece of corrugated iron, a piece of plastic, pieces of wire, a wooden stick, a block of wood, a piece of cloth, a candle, etc.

For you to try (page 68)

1 **Investigation: Showing air pressure (1)**
- A drinking glass and a piece of smooth cardboard.

2 **Investigation: Showing air pressure (2)**
- A glass or plastic drink bottle and a bucket of water.

For you to try (page 69)

1 **Investigation: Floating and sinking**
- A number of different materials such as small pieces of different kinds of timber (especially hardwoods), different metal objects, different kinds of stone including a piece of pumice, some cork and a bucket of water.

2 **Investigation: Peel the pomelo**
- A pomelo or grapefruit and a bucket of water.

3 **Investigation: Diver in a bottle**
- A large plastic bottle with a screw cap, a plastic pen top, some plasticine (or other weight) and a paper clip or piece of wire.

4 **Investigation: Paper boats**
- Several sheets of paper and some marbles or small stones.

For you to try (page 74)

1 **Investigation: Making and using an indicator**
- A few red hibiscus flowers, a tin can, plastic lid, different substances such as juice from a lemon (or other citrus fruits), some rain water, some vinegar, soap, toothpaste, shampoo, different cleaning materials such as Ajax, Bon Ami, some ash from a fire (mixed with water) etc.

Project: Make your own yogurt (page 77)
- A pot or saucepan, a vacuum flask, two bowls of different sizes, 250 mL of long-life milk and a small amount of plain yogurt. Students will also need to be able to use a refrigerator.

For you to try (page 81)

1 **Investigation: Conduction in solids**
- A small cooking pot and some different solids such as a 10-cm nail, a piece of fencing wire, a metal spoon, a plastic spoon, a wooden stick, an old biro case, the strap from an old rubber thong and a glass bottle.

2 **Investigation: Convection in liquids**
- A clear glass jar, hot water and something to colour the water like ink, dye, a little instant coffee powder, or the red colour from betel nut that has been mixed with lime.

For you to try (page 85)

1 **Investigation: Conductors and insulators**
- Two dry cells, a bulb and holder, several pieces of wire and some materials to test: metals such as a nail, an aluminium can and a piece of copper pipe, a glass marble, plastic, wood, stone, brick, paper etc.

2 **Investigation: Series and parallel**
- Two dry cells, three bulbs and holders, and eight pieces of wire.

For you to try (page 88)

1 **Investigation: Make an electromagnet**
- A large iron nail, a dry cell and about one metre of insulated wire and some paper clips.

2 **Investigation: Make a simple current meter**
- A new dry cell, an old dry cell, about one metre of insulated wire, a matchbox tray, a small compass and some plasticine or sticky tape.

For you to try (page 94)

1 **Investigation: Measuring forces**

- A thin strip of timber about 30 cm long, five D cells, a plastic bag or onion net, a piece of wire and a rubber band.

2 **Investigation: Measuring friction**

- A block of wood, a nail, a book, 30 marbles, some sand and the force-meter from the previous investigation.

Answers and explanations

For you to try (page 67)

1 **Investigation: Properties of matter**

Answers will vary depending on the materials that the students use, but some possible answers are suggested below:

Material	Strong	Hard	Brittle	Malleable	Ductile	Lustre	Transparent/ translucent	Conductor/ insulator	Density
rubber band	No	No	No	No	No	No	Opaque	Insulator—heat and electricity	Not dense
chalk	No	Yes	Yes	No	No	No	Opaque	Insulator—heat and electricity	Not dense
stone	Yes	Yes	No	No	No	No	Opaque	Insulator—heat and electricity	Dense
glass marble	Yes	Yes	No	No	No	Slightly	Partly transparent	Insulator—heat and electricity	Dense
aluminium can	Yes	Yes	No	Yes	Yes	Yes	Opaque	Conductor—heat and electricity	Dense
nail	Yes	Yes	No	No	Yes	Yes	Opaque	Conductor—heat and electricity	Dense
corrugated iron	Yes	Yes	No	Yes	No	Yes	Opaque	Conductor—heat and electricity	Dense
plastic	Yes	Yes	No	No	No	Slightly	Opaque	Insulator—heat and electricity	Not dense
pieces of wire	Yes	Yes	No	No	Yes	No	Opaque	Conductor—heat and electricity	Dense
wooden stick	Yes	Yes	No	No	No	No	Opaque	Insulator—heat and electricity	Not dense
block of wood	Yes	Yes	No	No	No	No	Opaque	Insulator—heat and electricity	Not dense
piece of cloth	No	No	No	No	No	No	Opaque	Insulator—heat and electricity	Not dense
candle	No	Yes	No	No	No	Slightly	Opaque	Insulator—heat and electricity	Not dense

For you to try (page 68)

1 **Investigation: Showing air pressure (1)**

- Students may be surprised to discover that the cardboard stays in place and the water does not fall out of the glass. The pressure of the air pushing against the cardboard, in this case acting upwards, is greater than the **weight** of the water which acts downwards.

2 Investigation: Showing air pressure (2)

- The water will not run out of the bottle as long as the neck is kept under the surface of the water in the bucket. The pressure of the air, in this case acting downwards, is greater than the weight of water that acts downwards.

For you to try (page 69)

1 Investigation: Floating and sinking

Answers will vary depending on the materials that the students use, but they should find that materials such as cork, pumice and most types of wood float but metal objects and some kinds of hardwood will sink in water.

2 Investigation: Peel the pomelo

- A pomelo or grapefruit will float in a bucket of water because the skin is very thick and full of trapped air bubbles. This makes the pomelo light for its size, so it floats. Without the skin and the air bubbles inside it, the pomelo weighs a lot more for its size. The peeled pomelo is more dense than water, so it sinks.

3 Investigation: Diver in a bottle

- The diver rises and sinks because there is a bubble of air trapped inside the pen top. This bubble of air makes the diver less dense than water so it floats.
- When you squeeze the bottle, water squashes the air inside the pen top into a smaller space which allows water to get inside the pen top. Now the diver is more dense than water so it sinks.
- When you relax your grip on the bottle, the air in the pen top expands again. Now the diver is less dense than the water, so it comes back up to the surface.

4 Investigation: Paper boats

- One method of making paper boats is shown but students may know others which will allow for some interesting comparisons to be made. Depending on the size and style of the boat and how well it is made, it should be able to carry several stones or marbles before sinking.

For you to try (page 72)

1 Answers will vary depending on the substances that the students choose, but some possible answers are suggested below:

Substance	Acidic	Basic	Neutral
Water			✓
Salt			✓
Soap		✓	
Betel nut	✓		
Lime powder		✓	
Lemon, lime	✓		
Toothpaste		✓	
Dry cell (inside)	✓		
Shampoo		✓	
Cleaning materials		✓	
Tea	✓		
Milk	✓		
Bleach		✓	

For you to try (page 74)

1 **Investigation: Making and using an indicator**
   - The indicator made from hibiscus flowers is red with acids and green with bases.
   - Acidic substances are the juice from lemons and other citrus fruits and vinegar. Rainwater may be slightly acidic or neutral.
   - Soap, toothpaste, and cleaning substances such as Ajax and Bon Ami, and ash from a fire (mixed with water) are usually basic. Shampoo may be slightly basic or neutral.

2 **Properties of acids:**
   - they have a sour taste
   - strong acids are very corrosive (should not be tasted)
   - they change the colour of indicators e.g. red litmus turns blue
   - they contain the element hydrogen
   - they can be used for cleaning metals

3 **Properties of bases:**
   - they are the opposite of acids
   - strong bases are very corrosive and can burn skin and makes holes in clothes
   - they change the colour of indicators e.g. litmus turns red
   - they make good cleaning agents

For you to try (page 76)

1 Some examples are as follows:
   a strong acids: hydrochloric acid, nitric acid, sulphuric acid
   b weak acids: citric acid, acetic acid
   c neutral solutions: pure water, salt solution
   d weak bases: shampoo, soap, toothpaste, most cleaning materials
   e strong bases: ammonium hydroxide, calcium hydroxide, sodium hydroxide

2 Gardeners and farmers sometimes add lime to soil when the soil is too acidic to grow crops well. It is especially added for crops that do not grow well in an acidic soil. The lime is basic and lowers the acidity of soil.

3 Examples of neutralisation from everyday life are:
   - Cleaning teeth with toothpaste. Toothpaste is basic and neutralises the acid in the mouth that destroys the enamel of teeth and can lead to tooth decay.
   - Chewing betel nut with lime. Betel nut is acidic and lime is basic and helps to neutralise the acid.
   - Adding lime to soil that is too acid. The lime is basic and neutralises the acidity of soil.

Project: Make your own yogurt (page 77)

- Making yogurt is a simple project if you have a vacuum flask, some long-life milk, some plain yogurt as a starter and the use of a refrigerator. This project demonstrates very nicely the effect of lactic acid produced by the bacteria. Teachers could also use this opportunity to discuss the importance of microbes such as bacteria. Although some bacteria are harmful and can make us sick, many are not harmful and some are useful.

For you to try (page 81)

1 **Investigation: Conduction in solids**

- Answers will vary depending on the solids that the students choose but metallic objects such as a nail, a piece of fencing wire, and a metal spoon, will be good conductors but a plastic spoon, a wooden stick, an old biro case, the strap from an old rubber thong and a glass bottle will be poor conductors.

2 **Investigation: Convection in liquids**

- When some colour is carefully added to the liquid at the side of the container it will begin to move in a circle from the top to the bottom of the container and back again. This current shows the movement of heat in a liquid and is known as convection.

3 Some examples where insulation is used in a house in order to keep it cool are as follows:

- Silver-coloured paper is placed under the corrugated iron of the roof to help reflect heat. One product or brand that is used in Papua New Guinea for this purpose is known as Sisalation.
- Having an air space between the ceiling and roof to act as insulation.
- Having an air space between the inside wall and outside wall to act as insulation.
- Using rolls of fibrous material to help improve the insulation in the roof or walls.

4 The heat from a fire makes the air hot and this rises up through the chimney of the stove with the smoke. A current of cooler air moves in to take the place of the hot air and this movement is called convection.

5 People making a mumu need to use insulators so that the heat from the hot stones does not escape but has time to cook the food. People usually use various leaves such as banana, hessian copra sacks and soil to cover the mumu.

6 In a place where the days are hot and sunny a suitable colour for a car would be white or some other light colour. A light colour will not absorb so much heat from the sun as a dark colour and this will help to keep the car cooler.

7 A chocolate flavoured ice-cream would melt more quickly on a sunny day than a plain white ice-cream because the dark colour of the chocolate flavoured ice-cream will absorb more heat from the sun.

8 A vacuum flask can be used to keep hot liquids hot and cold liquids cold because conduction, convection and radiation are reduced in the following ways:

- The walls are usually made of glass which is a poor conductor.
- The inner surfaces of the walls are shiny to prevent radiation.
- Air is removed from the space between the walls to make a vacuum which prevents conduction and convection.
- The stopper is made from a poor conductor such as cork, plastic or rubber.

9 Solids are made of many closely packed particles that are strongly held together but are also constantly moving or vibrating. When a solid is heated the particles vibrate faster. The vibrating particles are not able to move through a solid but the movement or vibration is passed on from particle to particle. In this way the heat vibrations of the particles are spread throughout the solid which is called conduction. In a gas the particles are much further apart and are not firmly held together. When the gas particles are heated they move further apart from each other and the gas expands rather than the vibration being passed from particle to particle as it does in a solid. For this reason conduction does not easily occur in gases.

For you to try (page 85)

1 **Investigation: Conductors and insulators**

- Metals such as a nail, an aluminium can and a piece of copper pipe will all conduct electricity. Non-metallic objects such as a glass marble, plastic, wood, stone, brick, paper are usually insulators and will not conduct electricity.

2 **Investigation: Series and parallel**

- When two or three bulbs are connected in series the brightness of each bulb decreases each time another bulb is added to the circuit. This is because the current does not increase but is shared by each bulb in the circuit.
- When two or three bulbs are connected in parallel the brightness of each bulb will stay the same each time another bulb is added to the circuit. This is because the same bulbs draw a bigger electric current each time a bulb is added and the same current flows in each part of the circuit. This also means that the battery will go flat more quickly.

3 Screwdrivers and pliers used by electricians usually have plastic handles and plastic covering the metal parts because plastic is a good insulator and helps to prevent electric shock. If the metal part of the screwdriver or pliers touches a wire or screw that is live or carrying electricity then the current will not be conducted to the hands of the person holding the tool. As a safety precaution an electrician will usually turn off the electricity to make sure that there is no current flowing in any part of the circuit.

4 **a** Most electrical appliances that we use in the home usually have at least two wires to make them work because two wires are needed to make a complete circuit.

b

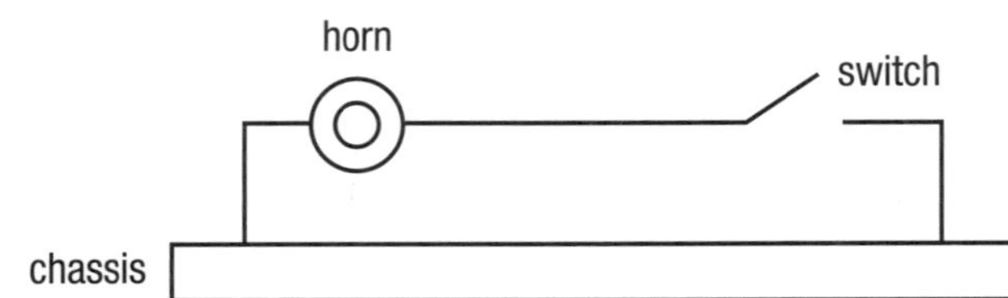

For you to try (page 88)

1 **Investigation: Make an electromagnet**

- When the wire is wound in a coil around the nail and a current is flowing in the wire, the nail inside will become an electromagnet and be able to pick up the paper clips.

2 **Investigation: Make a simple current meter**

- This simple experiment demonstrates the way that a meter works to measure an electric current.
- When the electricity is connected to the coil of wire the compass needle is moved by the magnetic effect of the electric current. The amount that the compass needle moves tells you about the size of the current—a big current will make the needle move more than a small current.
- A new dry cell will make the compass needle move more than the old dry cell because a new dry cell can produce a bigger current.
- When the wires are connected to the opposite **terminals** of the battery then the current flows in the opposite direction and so the compass needle will move in the opposite direction. This change in direction will occur with both the new dry cell and the old dry cell.

3 Thick copper wire is better than thin for use in connecting wires because although copper is a good conductor the thick wire has lower resistance. Nichrome wire should not be used for connecting wire because it is made from an alloy that is not a good conductor of electricity. Nichrome is a resistance wire that is used in heating elements.

For you to try (page 94)

1 **Investigation: Measuring forces**

- The force-meter is fairly easy to make and calibrate and answers will vary depending on the forces students choose to measure. The forces listed are only suggestions and students should be encouraged to choose their own as long as they are a suitable size that can be measured with their force-meter.

2 **Investigation: Measuring friction**

- A large force will be needed to move the block of wood.
- Placing the block of wood on some marbles will reduce the force needed to move it because the marbles act as ball bearings which reduce the area of contact and also roll and so reduce the friction.
- Placing a book on top of the block of wood on the floor will increase the forces needed to move the block because the weight of the book pushes down on the block and this has to be overcome before it will move.
- Spreading sand on the floor under the block may help to reduce the force needed to move the block because the particles of sand can act like small ball bearings. However, when there is a large force between the block and the floor, the roughness of the sand may increase the friction.

3 Answers will vary depending on the actions that the students choose but some suggestions follow.

Action	Push, pull or no force
Opening a window	push
Turning a screw with a screwdriver	push
Writing with a pencil	push and pull
Catching a fish	pull
Using a wheelbarrow	push
Getting water from a well	pull
Climbing a coconut tree	push and pull
Weeding the garden	pull
Cutting grass with a grass knife	push
Throwing a stone	push
Floating in water	no force (apart from **gravity**)
Sleeping in bed	no force (apart from gravity)

4 The four main types of forces are:
- gravitational forces e.g. the force of gravity that makes things fall downwards
- magnetic forces e.g. the magnet that is used to close the door of a fridge
- electrical forces e.g. the force in an electric motor that can make things move
- elastic forces e.g. the elastic force in the rubber of a spear gun used to catch fish.

5 **a** 1 newton
b 6 newtons
c 2.5 newtons
d 10 newtons
e 18 newtons

6 **a** 4 newtons
b 3.75 newtons

7 Answers will vary depending on the examples that the students choose but some examples are given below.
- Walking to school. The muscles of my legs used energy to make me move along the road. I also used energy to carry my school bag.
- Playing with friends. I used energy in my legs to run around and chase my friends. My arms also used energy to throw a ball to my friends and to catch the ball.
- Carrying firewood. I used energy in my arms and legs to look for the firewood, to lift it up and then carry it home.
- Climbing steps or stairs. I used energy in the muscles of my legs to overcome the force of gravity and get to the top of the steps or stairs.

8 Work is done when a force moves an object a certain distance. If something is not moving then no work is being done. When work is done, energy is used.

9 How many joules of energy are used in each of the following cases?
a work (J) = force (N) x distance (m) = 1 x 1 = 1 J
b work (J) = force (N) x distance (m) = 1 x 2 = 2 J
c work (J) = force (N) x distance (m) = 2 x 5 = 10 J
d work (J) = force (N) x distance (m) = 10 x 1 = 10 J

For you to try (page 99)

1 A simple machine is something that helps to make work easier such as a wheelbarrow. The main types of simple machines are:

- levers
- the wheel and axle
- **inclined planes**
- **pulleys**
- gear wheels.

Key
p = pivot
e = effort
l = load
e.d. = effort distance
l.d. = load distance

2

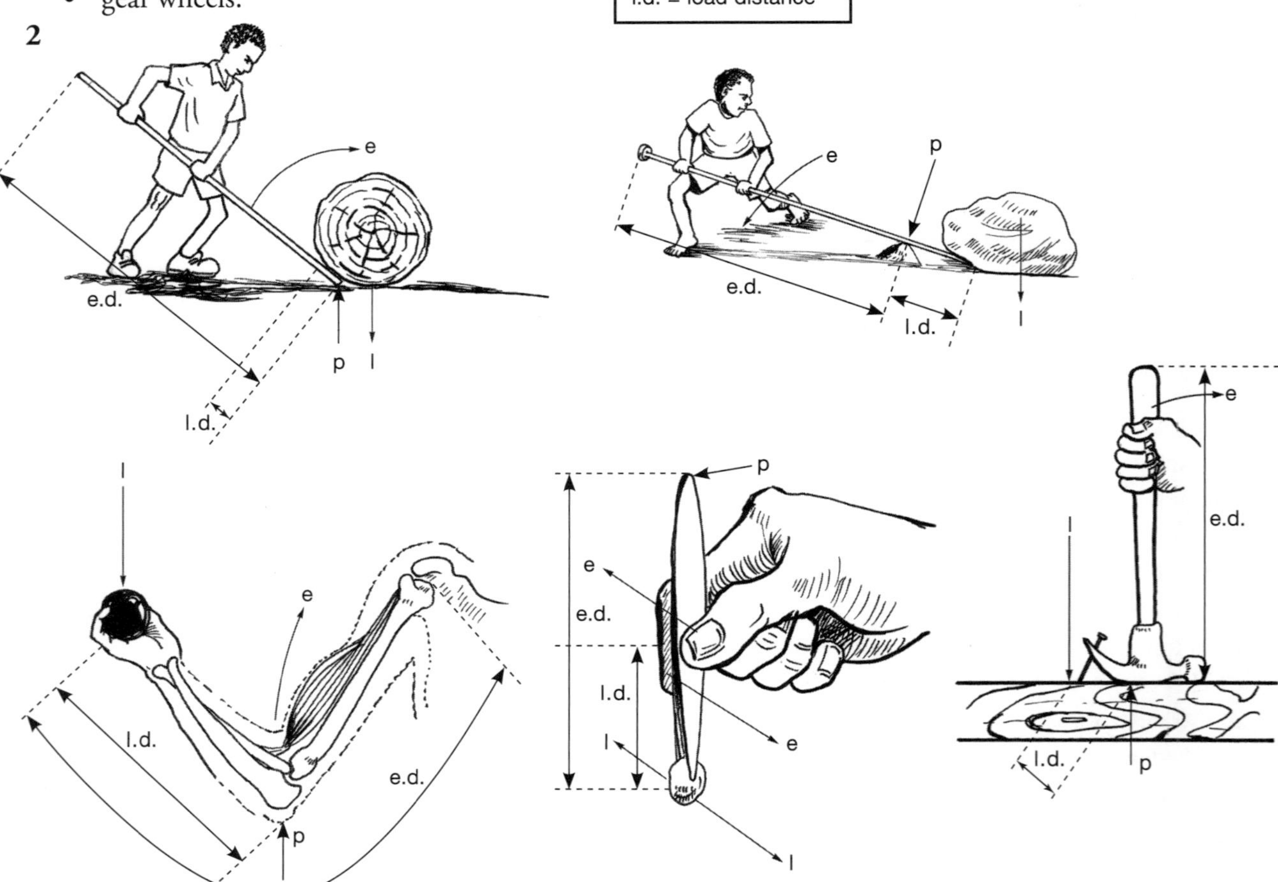

3 Answers will vary but some examples are: a bottle opener, scissors, bamboo tongs, forceps or tweezers, screwdriver, door handle, steps and stairs, the pulley on a bucket shower.

4 work (J) = force (N) x distance (m) = 20 x 5 = 100 J

5 work (J) = force (N) x distance (m) = 400 x 3 = 1200 J

6 Visiting a wharf or building site should enable students to see pulleys being used in a crane to lift cargo or building materials. Visiting a garage or workshop should allow students to see a **block and tackle** being used to lift an engine, gearbox or body parts such as the tray of a utility.

For you to try (page 101)

1 When we use a simple machine we put in a force and the machine puts out a force that does the job. Many simple machines give a force advantage. In other words they put out more force than you put in. However, the output movement is less than the input movement. We can see this more clearly when we try to move an object with a weight using a lever. The output force is greater than the input force, but only moves a smaller distance. In a lever the energy output is equal to the energy input. This means that the lever wastes no energy, so its efficiency is 100%. However, most machines waste energy

because of friction in their moving parts. Some energy is also lost as heat. In other words the energy output is less than the energy input.

This means their efficiency is less than 100%. For example, the efficiency of a diesel engine is about 35% and the efficiency of a petrol engine is about 25%.

2 It is better to use fluorescent tubes or bulbs for lighting rather than filament light bulbs because the efficiency of fluorescent tubes and bulbs is about 20% whereas the efficiency of filament light bulbs is 3%. This means that fluorescent tubes and bulbs give more light for the amount of electricity that they use and they cost less to use.

3 It is important for engines and power stations to have the highest possible efficiency because the cost of fuel has to be paid for by the people using the engine or the electricity. Most people want the cost to be as low as possible and a more efficient engine or power station will help to reduce the cost.

Summary questions

1

	Meaning	Physical property		Answer
A	Bends easily and can be hammered into shape	Brittle	I	C
B	Can be pulled out into wires	Conductor	II	D
C	**Hard**, but can break easily	Dense	III	K
D	Lets heat or electricity pass through easily	Ductile	IV	B
E	Lets some light through, but scatters it	Hard	V	F
F	Not easily scratched or worn away	Lustre	VI	I
G	Resists the effects of forces	Insulator	VII	J
H	'See-through' or lets light through very easily	Malleable	VIII	A
I	Shiny or lustrous	Transparent	IX	H
J	Stops heat or electricity passing through	Translucent	X	E
K	The amount of matter in a given space—dense objects sink in water	Strong	XI	G

2 A
3 C
4 D
5 A
6 B
7 C
8 A
9

	Force	Rank
A	A truck hitting a pole	4
B	An aeroplane taking off	5
C	Threading cotton through the eye of a needle	1
D	Kicking a ball	2
E	Pushing a car along the road	3

10 D
11 C
12 D
13 C
14 A
15 D
16 C
17 The materials that we use every day have different physical **properties** such as hardness, strength and density. When we use **materials** we choose those that have the most suitable properties. For example, some things will **float** and some things will sink. Some substances have different **chemical** properties. For example, some things are **acids** and some things are bases. Acidic and basic substances can be found in **nature** and are used by people in different ways. Acids and **bases** can also be made and used in everyday life.

When we use **energy** in the home we often use heat energy and electrical energy. Heat is a **form** of energy that can make substances hot and can be controlled. Temperature is a **measure** of how hot a substance is. Electricity has three main uses or **effects**—heating, lighting and magnetism. Electricity must flow around a path called a **circuit** which we can draw as a diagram. Simple machines can help people to do work because there is a **mechanical** advantage. We can calculate the amount of work that we do and the mechanical advantage of different **machines**.

STRAND 4 Earth and beyond

About this strand

This strand builds on the ideas in basic geology and astronomy that were introduced in Grade 6 and 7. It consists of two sub-strands. The first sub-strand **Our Earth and its origin** begins by looking at rocks and their importance through the three main stages of development that have occurred in some parts of the world—the stone age, bronze age and iron age. Students are reminded about the formation of different kinds of rocks and they find out more about **igneous rocks**, especially mineral composition, crystal size and how they can be classified. The formation of **metamorphic rocks** due to pressure and heat is also covered in greater detail. The importance of minerals is developed by looking at the metals that can be obtained from **mineral ores**. The topic goes on to look briefly at ways of searching for metals and extracting metals. The first sub-strand concludes by looking at the importance of minerals in Papua New Guinea.

In the second sub-strand, **Space exploration**, students find out about various **satellites** of the Earth and their different uses. The strand develops by looking at the unmanned exploration of **space** and the steps taken to make it possible to send the first humans into space. The space shuttle is described together with its uses, for example, in servicing the international **space station**, and this leads to a description of the challenges of living in space. The final topic in this strand uses various methods of looking into space with different types of **telescopes** to introduce the broader idea of the process of communication through telephone, radio and television as well as through satellites.

Sub-strands 1 and 2

Main ideas

Sub-strand 1: All rocks are made of minerals and the properties of a rock depend on the minerals that it contains. The slow cooling of **magma** produces igneous rock with large crystals, while the fast cooling of magma produces igneous rock with small crystals. Metamorphic rocks have been changed by heat and pressure. Rocks can be classified according to the minerals that they contain, the size of the crystals and they way that we use them. Metals can be obtained from minerals and the extraction of metals from rocks known as ores is important in Papua New Guinea.

Sub-strand 2: Satellites orbiting the Earth are used for many different purposes. Space was first explored using unmanned satellites and probes. People have landed on the Moon and also live on an international space station orbiting the Earth. Telephone, radio and television are important methods of communication.

Key words

Stone age, bronze age, iron age, minerals, elements, compounds, ores, magma, igneous, **fissure**, intrusive, extrusive, **obsidian**, **basalt**, pumice, **granite**, dolerite, sedimentary, metamorphic, **hornfels**, **marble**, rim of fire, alluvial, **placer deposit**, **panning**, **geostationary satellite**, **space probe**, space shuttle, **heavenly bodies**, astronomy, telescope, communication, telephone, radio, television.

Key facts

- All rocks are made of minerals. The way a rock looks and its properties depend on the minerals that make the rock.
- Rock can be formed in different ways—igneous, sedimentary and metamorphic.
- Igneous rocks are formed by the cooling of molten rock called magma.
- Slow cooling produces large crystals, while fast cooling produces small crystals.
- Igneous rocks can be classified according to crystal size, minerals and colour.
- **Sedimentary rocks** are formed from broken down rock that is eroded and carried by rivers to the sea where it collects and becomes cemented together again.
- Metamorphic rocks are rocks that have been changed.
- Metamorphic rocks can be formed by heat and pressure. The type of metamorphic rock produced depends on the amount of heat, the amount of pressure and the type of original rock.
- Rocks can be classified according to the minerals that they contain, the size of the crystals and the way that we use them.
- Metals can be obtained from minerals and the extraction of metals from rocks known as ores is important in Papua New Guinea.
- We use satellites orbiting the Earth in space to transmit radio, television and telephone messages to any part of the world. Satellites are important in communication.
- We can find out more about space by using different kinds of telescopes.
- People have travelled through space to the Moon and there is an international space station orbiting the Earth which a few people from different countries visit for short periods of time.

Assessment tasks

Assessment aims to gather information on how well students have achieved the outcomes of the strand. A variety of strategies should be used: written, oral and practical.

Each assessment item should be based on criteria that have been clearly written down. Students should be told what the criteria are so that they know the basis for judgment of their achievement and demonstration of the outcomes.

Assessment should also be continuous and collected throughout the learning process by the completion of appropriate activities such as those indicated with the assessment icon in the 'For you to try' sections.

Major links to other subjects

Strand 4: Earth and beyond builds upon ideas introduced in Culture and Community at the elementary level and Environmental Studies at the lower primary level. At the upper primary level, **Earth and beyond** links to the strand **Our culture, lifestyle and values** in Personal Development. Aspects of different subjects can be integrated into activities such as:

- a project to improve life in the community
- collecting and analysing statistical data for specific groups in the community
- designing posters or performing a drama to relay the message of the benefits of using the methods of science.

Links with other subjects are noted with an **icon** in the student books.

Teacher information

Brief information is provided on the formation of sedimentary and metamorphic rock but this is for the sake of completion and as a background since the main emphasis is the formation of different types of igneous rocks. This leads to the formation of rocks known as mineral ores and the ways that metals can be obtained from minerals.

Rocks and their importance

This topic uses a historical approach to describe the way that people have learned to use rocks and then extract metals from rocks beginning with the stone age and then moving on through the bronze age and iron age.

It is important to understand the three ages did not happen in every part of the world and did not happen at the same time in different places. The dates in the table are approximate and cover the time periods in different places. However, scientists have enough information from different parts of the world to understand the way in which people slowly learned to make different metals from rocks. As people began to travel more and methods of communication improved so more people found out about the ways of making and using different kinds of metals.

Minerals

This topic can also be linked to the following sub-strands:

8.2.2 Draw conclusions about the effects of excessive use of non-biodegradable material on food webs, especially in relation to the topic Renewable and non-renewable materials (p.55)

8.3.1 Conduct investigations and use collected data to identify patterns in the physical interactions of substances, especially in relation to the topic Properties of materials (p.66)

For example, all the metals in the table below are also elements.

Some mineral ores and their related metals	
Mineral ores	**Metal obtained**
haematite	iron
limonite	iron
bauxite	aluminium
chalcopyrite	copper
azurite	copper
galena	lead
cinnabar	mercury
cassiterite	tin
carnonite	uranium

Students should not be expected to remember the names of mineral ores but rather to understand the basic principle of obtaining metals from ores.

Igneous rocks

There are two main types of igneous rock that are formed when magma cools and solidifies.

- Intrusive igneous rocks are formed inside the Earth when the magma goes solid before it reaches the surface. This is the most common type of igneous rock.
- Extrusive igneous rocks are formed when the magma reaches the surface of the Earth through a volcano or flows through a deep crack called a fissure and then cools and solidifies.

Classifying igneous rocks

The table below summarises the formation and classification of different types of igneous rock:

Formation and classification of igneous rocks				
Speed of cooling of magma	**Crystal size**	**Light coloured rock → dark coloured rock (e.g. the continents → under the oceans)**		
Fast e.g. extrusive	Small crystals Fine grain	Rhyolite	**Andesite**	Basalt
Slow e.g. intrusive	Large crystals Coarse grain	Granite	Diorite	Gabbro

Sedimentary rocks

Brief information is provided on the formation of sedimentary rock but this is mainly revision, and for the sake of completion, since it was covered in more detail in Grade 7 together with fossils.

Metamorphic rocks

Brief information is provided on the formation of metamorphic rock due to pressure and heat but this is more for the sake of completion and as a background since the main emphasis is the formation of different types of igneous rocks and the importance of minerals.

The importance of minerals in Papua New Guinea

Money earned from the mining of minerals is important to the economy of Papua New Guinea and minerals exploration and mining is controlled by the Department of Mining and Petroleum. The government is able to do this because although the people own the land, the minerals that are found twenty metres or more below the surface belong to the government or state.

Looking for minerals and starting a mine is a business that involves a lot of risk and the investment of large amounts of money. Mining companies often spend millions of kina searching for minerals which they may not find. When they do find minerals, scientists must measure or estimate the size of the **ore body** and measure how much metal is present in the ore. The amount of metal present is calculated as a percentage and is usually very small. Using this information and calculating the cost of setting up the mine and extracting the metal together with the price of metals on the world market means a decision may then be made to set up the mine. In many cases a mine is not set up because the amount of metal in the ore is too low, the ore body is too small or the cost of setting up the mine and extracting the metal is too high in relation to the money that can be earned from selling the metal.

The lifetime of a mine is also important and must be calculated. For example, gold was first mined on Misima over one hundred years ago but stopped when the gold that was easy to find and extract was finished. The most recent Misima gold mine began in 1989 and mining stopped in 2001 although gold was still processed until 2004. This means that the life of the mine was fifteen years, which was calculated before the mine started. This way landowners can also be informed about the life of the mine.

The PNG Chamber of Mines and Petroleum helps to coordinate the activities of the mining and petroleum sector and is a good source of information. They have produced learning materials for use in schools and have their own website.

Space exploration

This sub-strand makes the link between using different kinds of rocks and metal ores obtained from rocks on the Earth and exploring beyond the Earth and into space.

The idea of natural satellites of the Earth, such as the Moon that was introduced in Grade 7, is extended to include artificial satellites.

Unmanned exploration of space

The table on page 124 of the Student Book summarises some of the main unmanned probes in space exploration. Many of the probes were part of a series with the same name rather than just a single probe. Although there have been other probes the ones that are described are sufficient to give a clear picture of what happened. The unmanned exploration of space is continuing and over the next few years, teachers should also look for news about the following two space probes:

Name of probe	Date	Purpose
Phoenix (USA)	2008	Expected to land on Mars and explore below the surface
New Horizons (USA)	2006–15	Fly by Jupiter in 2007, fly by Pluto in 2015, then leave the **solar system**

Humans in space

The exploration of space will continue and teachers will need to read newspapers and listen to the radio to keep up to date with the latest developments of both existing programs and new programs. For example, in September 2007, the space shuttle flew into space again and visited the International Space Station. At the same time the Japanese also announced that they will begin their own space program to send people to the Moon. Other countries such as India and China have also announced plans to have a space program.

Because much of the equipment and technology used on the space shuttle is now thirty years old and out of date the space shuttle will not be used after 2010. It will be replaced by Orion which is a new spacecraft that will take humans to the Moon and beyond. Teachers should also look out for news about this project.

Looking into space

In order to make the telescope teachers will need to obtain suitable lenses and students may need help to make the telescope. Obtaining suitable lenses may be difficult in some places and it may not be possible to make more than one telescope but it is worth making the effort to make at least one, in which case it could become a class project rather than an investigation.

Communication

This topic makes the link between using satellites for various types of communication as the main step in the process of communication and more general examples of communication.

One of the fastest growing methods of communication is the Internet which allows people to obtain information from the World Wide Web (www). In order to communicate in this way people must have a computer and be able to connect to the Internet using a telephone line or satellite. When people are connected to the Internet it is possible to type and send electronic letters called email to anywhere in the world and get a reply straightaway. People can also use earphones and a microphone to talk to each other over the Internet, and it is also possible to use a special camera called a web cam so that people can see each other as they talk.

The Internet can also be used to find information, which is like looking in a library, but it is much quicker and much more information is available than in a library. People can also buy things over the Internet, book airline tickets, pay their bills and even do their banking.

Equipment needed for the activities and investigations

To complete the investigations and activities in this chapter each group of students will need the following.

For you to try (page 112)

1 Investigation: Using stones

- Stone tools such as an axe, adze, a scraper and some mumu stones.

Project: Panning for gold (page 120)

An old large frying pan and a small plastic container with a lid.
Access to a local creek or river.

Project: Making fishing weights

Old batteries, short pieces of fencing wire, an old pot or saucepan, betel nut skin.

For you to try (page 130)

1 Investigation: Making a simple telescope

- Two cardboard or plastic tubes and two different convex lenses or magnifying glasses (convex lenses are thicker in the centre than at the edge).
- Plasticine or sticky tape to fix the lenses in the tube and polystyrene foam blocks to hold the smaller tube inside the bigger tube.

2 Investigation: Observing the Sun

- The telescope from Investigation 1 (above) and a piece of white paper or cardboard.

For you to try (page 135)

1 Investigation: Making a string telephone

- Two clean tin cans without sharp edges and a length of string. A hammer and a nail.

Answers and explanations

For you to try (page 112)

1 Investigation: Using stones

- A stone axe is used to cut down trees. The stone that is chosen must be able to be sharpened by rubbing on another stone and it may be sharpened on both sides to make a wedge shape. The stone is fixed into a wooden handle in such a way that the cutting edge of it is usually in the same plane as the direction of the force that is applied through the handle. The stone chosen is usually an igneous rock that is hard enough to be sharpened without breaking into small pieces, but not too hard, as this would make it very difficult to sharpen.
- A stone adze is used to hollow out a canoe. The stone that is chosen must be able to be sharpened by rubbing on another stone and it is usually sharpened only on one side to make a wedge shape. The stone is fixed into a wooden handle in such a way that the cutting edge is usually at right angles to the direction of the force that is applied through the handle. The stone chosen is usually an igneous rock that is hard enough to be sharpened without breaking into small pieces, but not too hard, as this would make it very difficult to sharpen.
- A stone scraper is used to hollow out a wooden bowl or to scrape food. The stone is usually a size that can easily be held in the hand. The stone chosen is usually an igneous rock that is hard enough to be sharpened without breaking into small pieces, but not too hard as this would make it very difficult to sharpen.
- Mumu stones are stones that are heated very strongly in a fire and then used to cook food in a ground oven. The stones should be able to be heated for a long time without breaking and should not cool down quickly but hold their heat. They should be a size that can be picked up easily with bamboo

tongs—not too big or too small. The stones chosen are usually igneous rocks that have been moving along the bed of a river so that they are quite rounded and smooth to touch.

2 Igneous rocks are formed from molten rocks called magma that cools down deep inside the Earth. Magma that cools down inside the Earth forms intrusive igneous rock. However, when magma reaches the surface of the Earth through a volcano or flows through a deep crack called a fissure and then cools down, extrusive igneous rocks are formed.

3 Magma is the name of the molten rock that is found deep in the Earth. When it comes to the surface and escapes through a volcano or a deep crack called a fissure, then it is called lava.

4 **a** Pumice is a type of igneous rock that is very light and can float on water.
   b Pumice is likely to be found washed up on beaches in areas where there are volcanoes.
   c Pumice is formed when gases dissolved in the rock are released when the lava erupts at the surface through a volcano. The lava hardens very quickly and bubbles of gas form many small holes in the rock.
   d Pumice stone can be used to clean things and to rub on your skin to make it soft or clean it. Pumice can also be used to smooth the bottom of a canoe or to make wood smooth before painting it.

5 • Igneous rocks that have cooled quickly have small crystals and are said to be fine-grained.
   • Igneous rocks that have cooled slowly have large crystals and are said to be coarse-grained.

6 Igneous rocks such as granite are very hard with closely packed crystals and can be polished easily. For this reason they can be used to make buildings and for making monuments and headstones for graves. Although New York City is a very modern city it still has many old pavements or sidewalks that are made from big slabs of granite about 3 metres by 3 metres and 200 millimetres thick. Many of these sidewalks were laid down when the city was developed 160 years ago.

7 The characteristics that are used to classify igneous rocks are crystal size or grain and colour.

For you to try (page 114)

1 Metamorphic rocks can be formed in two main ways.

- By pressure due to movement in the Earth's crust that creates great pressure within the rocks of the crust and can make rocks change. The minerals may be flattened and pushed into layers.
- By heat, for example when magma comes into contact with them. When rocks are heated the materials within the rock may be changed. This type of metamorphosis is called contact metamorphism and hornfels is a typical rock that is made in this way.

2 Slate is a metamorphic rock that is produced when movement in the Earth's crust creates great pressure that changes the original rocks such as shale or mudstone.

Slate splits easily because the original shale and mudstone are both sedimentary rocks that were created when the **sediments** were laid down in layers. The pressure forces the particles very close together so that after they have hardened they form layers which are so strong that they can be split into sheets.

Split sheets of slate can be easily used to make roof tiles and floors of houses. Slate roof tiles are not heavy and can be drilled and nailed on to the wooden frame of the roof. Slate is also used to make pool tables because a big sheet of slate is flat and smooth.

3 Marble is metamorphic rock that is formed when limestone is changed by heat and pressure. Marble is a hard rock but it can be cut and polished and used to make floors, and it is also used to make walls in bathrooms and benches in kitchens. However, it is very expensive so many people do not use it. Some of the hotels in Port Moresby have marble bathrooms. Marble can also be used to make statues. Marble sometimes contains fossils because the original rock is limestone which is the sedimentary rock in which fossils are often found. However, many of the fossils may have been destroyed by heat.

4 **a** Granite is an igneous rock that can be cut into slabs or blocks but cannot be split into sheets. It is very strong and not easily spoilt by the weather. Its main disadvantage is that it is very heavy and

a granite roof could not easily be supported by a wooden frame. For this reason it is not normally used to make a roof.

b Limestone is a sedimentary rock formed from layers of sediment and can be split with some difficulty into thick sheets. It may be possible to support such a roof with a wooden frame but it would need to be strong because the roof would be much heavier than slate. Another disadvantage is the fact that limestone can slowly dissolve in rainwater so the roof may eventually begin to crack and leak.

5 Many graves that are made of stone are made from granite, which can vary in colour from brown to grey and even black. Many of these gravestones are highly polished and can look very shiny. Some gravestones are made of marble. These are usually much lighter in colour—white or cream.

For you to try (page 119)

1 Answers will vary but some suggestions are given below:
Bucket, saucepans, enamel plates, mugs, knives, forks, spoons, scissors, kerosene stove, hurricane lamp, coins, bush knife, axe, netball rings, goal posts, old gas cylinder used as a bell, spear from spear gun, fishing hooks, louvre frames, flywire, flagpole, fencing wire, Marsden matting left from World War II etc.

2 Metals are useful because they have a wide range of properties and can be made into a wide variety of objects. Many metals are strong, rigid, malleable, ductile and durable. Different metals can be mixed together to make alloys with more useful properties. Metals can be cast into many different shapes, made into sheets and pipes and stretched into wires to make springs, fences and carry electricity. Metals can be sharpened to make tools and also used to make many different kinds of fasteners such as nails, screws, nuts and bolts.

3

A bush materials roof versus a corrugated iron roof	
Advantages	**Disadvantages**
Low cost or no cost	Cannot be used to collect rainwater
Keeps the house much cooler	Can be destroyed by insects
Looks more attractive	Fire risk—can easily burn
Easy to erect	Can only last for a few years
Uses renewable resources	

4 Minerals are very important in Papua New Guinea because the government is able to earn a lot of money from the goods that are sold overseas. In 2005 about half the money that the government earned came from metals obtained from the mining of minerals. This is possible because Papua New Guinea is part of the Pacific rim of fire and has a lot of mineral resources. Because the minerals under the ground are owned by the state the government is able to control the way in which these resources are used.

5 Rocks and minerals that are mined from the ground are a non-renewable resource because although there may be a lot of these resources there is fixed amount which cannot be replaced. (Although the changes occurring inside the Earth that cause earthquakes and volcanoes can also bring rocks containing metal ores close to the surface this does not mean that minerals are renewable.)

For you to try (page 129)

1 Answers will vary and students may concentrate on the unmanned exploration of space, exploration involving humans or both.

2 Answers will vary depending on the dates that the students choose. One of the important skills is to be able to choose and use a suitable scale.

3 Answers will vary depending on the information that the students choose to include on the plate and this should lead to some lively group discussion of the most important things about human life on Earth and the best way to represent and communicate this information. Students will need to remember that if intelligent living things do exist on other planets, they will not look like humans or speak human languages so they will need to think carefully about the information to include and how to show this information.

The most obvious part of the information on the plate that was fixed to Pioneer showed two drawings that humans would recognise as a man and a woman from a European background. They were shown against a diagram of the Pioneer spacecraft itself to give some idea of scale. The man was taller than the woman, which is normally the case, although not always. The man was holding up one hand and appeared to be waving, but the idea of waving as a greeting may not be shared by other intelligent living things. Also the man and woman were both naked. Of course most people do not go around naked, but normally wear clothes. However, the clothes that people wear vary enormously depending on age, sex, culture, the activity they are doing and time of the year. There was much discussion about this at the time and not everybody agreed but in the end it was decided that it was clearer and less confusing to show them naked.

Another part of the diagram on the Pioneer plate also showed our solar system and the route taken by the spacecraft before it left our solar system.

There are no easy or correct answers to the challenge of choosing and communicating information such as this but students should be able to make their own choices and give reasons.

4

- The main problem of living in space would be weightlessness. Because there is no gravity everything floats about unless it is fixed. Weightlessness also affects the way the human body works.
- Food would be dried food and water would be added before it is eaten. The food would need to be healthy, nutritious, light in weight and not easily break into small pieces that would float about in the space station.
- Water would be drunk through a special cup with lid and straw so that it did not float about. Some water would be carried from Earth but water would also be made from oxygen and hydrogen. Urine would also be collected and made pure so the water could be used again.
- Going to the toilet would be quite difficult. A special vacuum toilet would be used that has arms which hold the person on to the seat and then the waste would be sucked into a plastic bag.
- Having a bath would also be a problem because washing in the normal way would mean that the water would just float about everywhere. A wet cloth or sponge would be used instead to have a sponge bath.
- Exercise would be difficult because of the weightlessness but it is needed for at least two hours every day in order to stay fit and healthy. A special exercise machine like a stationary bicycle or a rowing machine would be used.

For you to try (page 130)

1 Investigation: Making a simple telescope

- The method of operation of the telescope in this investigation is similar to many commercially produced telescopes.
- However, the image will appear to be upside down because two lenses are used. Most telescopes that you buy use more than two lenses so that the image then appears the right way round.
- When the instructions are followed this investigation will produce a working telescope but it will need some trial and error and adjustment in order to be able to focus and make the image as clear as possible.

2 Investigation: Observing the Sun

- It is safe to observe the Sun by holding your telescope so the image falls on a piece of white paper or cardboard. However, students should be warned never to look at the Sun with telescopes or binoculars because it is bright enough to damage the eyes.

For you to try (page 135)

1 Investigation: Making a string telephone

- The simple string telephone will only work when the string is pulled tight so that the sound vibrations can be conducted from particle to particle along the string. This means that both people must hold the can tightly or it will be pulled out of their hands by the other person. At the same time each person must hold the can to the mouth or ear in order to talk or listen. They may need to arrange some signal to let the other person know that they have finished speaking and are ready to listen to the reply. One way of doing this is to say 'over'.
- The sound will reduce with a longer string but a very long string will be difficult to pull tight because of the weight of the string. This will depend on the type of string that is used.
- Students can try to talk to a person who is round a corner—for example, one person at the side of a building and the other at the back. The string can be kept taut by pulling against the corner of the building but the sound will not be transmitted because when the string is touching something it interrupts the sound vibrations.

Summary questions

1 A

Statement about minerals	True of false?
Minerals are the chemical elements and chemical compounds that make up rocks.	T
There are many different minerals and all are easy to find.	F
Most rocks are made of minerals but some are not.	F
The way a rock looks and its properties depend on the minerals that make up the rock.	T
Most rocks are a mixture of a few minerals.	T
Landowners in PNG also own all the minerals below the ground.	F

3 B

4 A

5 C

6

	Description	Examples of use	Rock
I	Very hard, sparkles due to minerals	Building, making roads	C
II	Light colour, not hard	Building, used in cement and concrete	A
III	Light colour, hard, smooth	Building, statues	B
IV	Hard but splits into flat sheets	Roofing tiles, pool table	D

7

Statement	True or false?
Igneous rock comes from magma that has cooled and solidified.	T
Different igneous rocks found in different parts of the world contain different minerals.	T
Igneous rocks can be classified by the type of minerals they contain and by the size of the crystals of the minerals.	T
Igneous rocks with small crystals have cooled slowly.	F
Igneous rocks with large crystals have cooled quickly.	F

8 A

9 A

10

Activity affected by gravity?	True or false?
Using **solar** cells to obtain electricity	F
Moving about and taking exercise	T
Eating and drinking	T
Having a bath	T
Going to the toilet	T
Bringing all rubbish back to the Earth	F

11 D

12 All rocks are made of **minerals**. The way a **rock** looks and its properties depend on the minerals that make the rock. Rock can be **formed** in different ways—igneous, sedimentary and metamorphic. Igneous rocks are formed by the **cooling** of molten rock called magma. Slow cooling produces large **crystals**, while fast cooling produces small crystals. Igneous rocks can be classified according to crystal **size**, minerals and colour. Sedimentary rocks are formed from broken down rock that is **eroded** and carried by rivers to the sea where it collects and becomes cemented together again.

Metamorphic rocks are rocks that have been changed. Metamorphic rocks can be formed by **heat** and pressure. The type of metamorphic rock produced depends on the amount of heat, the amount of **pressure** and the type of original rock.

Rocks can be **classified** according to the minerals that they contain, the size of the crystals and the way that we use them. Metals can be obtained from minerals and the extraction of metals from rocks known as **ores** is important in Papua New Guinea.

We use **satellites** orbiting the Earth in space to transmit radio, television and telephone messages to any part of the world. Satellites are important in **communication**. We can find out more about **space** by using different kinds of telescopes. People have travelled through space to the **Moon** and there is an international space station orbiting the Earth which a few people from different countries visit for short periods of time.

Appendices

Sample unit of work

This unit of work is just one way of integrating a number of learning outcomes from different strands and sub-strands of science in Grade 8. There are many ways that teachers can integrate learning outcomes, including from other subjects, to make a unit of work. Teachers need to develop units of work that meet the needs of the students and the community, and also suit their own teaching style. Just as we weave bilums from different kinds of material into different shapes and sizes to be used for different purposes, so different units of work can be planned and implemented, each with their own individual characteristics.

Sample unit

Title: Using energy in the home

Grade: 8

Time frame: Eight weeks

Strand: Science in the home

Sub-strands:

- Apply their knowledge about energy to investigate electrical and heat energy in the home (8.3.3)
- Apply their knowledge about force to investigate simple machines (8.3.4)
- Conduct investigations on simple machines and use problem-solving skills to establish the efficiency of the machine as a tool to do work (8.3.5)

Purpose of the unit of work: to develop an understanding of the concept of energy and the way that energy can be used to do work in the community and make life easier.

Suggested links with other subjects or strands within Science:

Personal Development: Strand: Our Culture, Lifestyle and Values

Social Science: Strand: Culture

Process skills	Student activities	Assessment	Number of lessons and estimated time
Investigating	• Identify and describe real-life situations in the community where methods of applying and controlling heat are used to improve the standard of living • Design an investigation to demonstrate a practical application of using and controlling heat • Design, construct and test different types of electrical circuits • Investigate how forces are applied in a simple machine in order to make it move and change direction • Demonstrate how a lever can be applied to move a heavy object • Find out how different forces are measured • Make a simple force-meter and use it to measure the forces needed to move suitable objects • Design and carry out an investigation to find out about the efficiency of a simple machine such as a lever • Conduct a survey to identify how simple machines can be used to do work	**Assessment task** List and classify different applications of heat energy. Write up a Scientific Report of an experiment or investigation on the application of heat energy. Write up a Scientific Report of an experiment or investigation on making and using a simple force-meter. Write up a Scientific Report of an experiment or investigation to demonstrate the efficiency of a simple machine such as a lever. **Assessment criteria** The student correctly lists and describes different applications of heat energy. Student satisfactorily designs and writes up an investigation using the headings Aim, Apparatus, Method, Results, and Conclusion.	10 × 40-minute lessons for activities 3 × 30-minute lessons for assessment
Comprehending	• Explain real-life situations in the community where methods of applying and controlling heat are used to improve the standard of living • Evaluate results of experiments involving electrical circuits • Calculate the mechanical advantage of simple machines using the simple formula MA = Load / Effort • Calculate work done using the simple formula Work = Force × Distance • Calculate the efficiency of a simple machine using the formula Efficiency = Energy output / Energy input (× 100%) • Evaluate the results of investigations and make changes based on findings • Analyse findings from a survey on how simple machines can be used to do work	**Assessment task** Identify or describe situations in which heat is applied and controlled. Use a simple formula to calculate the mechanical advantage of simple machines. Use a simple formula to calculate the work done by simple machines. Gather, summarise and interpret information from a survey on the use of simple machines. **Assessment criteria** The student correctly identifies or describes examples of applying and controlling heat. Student correctly calculates the mechanical advantage, work done and efficiency of simple machines. Student satisfactorily gathers, summarises and interprets survey information.	10 × 40-minute lessons for activities 3 × 30-minute lessons for assessment

Communicating	• Describe how forces are applied in a simple machine in order to make it move and change direction • Explain the forces involved in using a lever to move a heavy object • Make recommendations based on analysis of findings from the survey	**Assessment task** Produce a labelled diagram or poster to describe how forces are applied in a simple machine to make it move and change direction. Analyse survey findings and make suitable recommendations. **Assessment criteria** Student chooses a suitable example, produces a clear diagram or poster, with appropriate heading and labels that communicates a message effectively. Student satisfactorily analyses findings from the survey and makes recommendations that are clearly related to the findings.	10 × 40-minute lessons for activities 3 × 30-minute lessons for assessment

Resources: *National Curriculum Statement, Science Upper Primary Syllabus 2003. Science Upper Primary Teachers Guide 2000, Grade 8 Student Book.*

Total estimated time for the unit of work: 30 x 40-minute teaching periods; 9 x 30-minute periods for assessment. (Total: 1470 minutes i.e. approximately the equivalent of eight weeks of work for science.)

Planning templates

Following are some sample templates that can be used for both long- and short-term planning.

Sample 1: Yearly plan

Units of work	Term 1	Term 2	Term 3	Term 4
Working scientifically	The scientific method	The scientific method	The scientific method	The scientific method
Living things	The process of reproduction and the effect of the environment	The process of reproduction and the effect of the environment	Effects of non-biodegradable materials on food webs	Effects of non-biodegradable materials on food webs
Science in the home	Patterns in the physical interaction of substances	Basic and acidic substances and their use in the community	Electrical and heat energy in the home	Simple machines, mechanical advantage and efficiency
Earth and beyond	Igneous and metamorphic rocks	Obtaining metals from minerals	Human exploration of space	Human exploration of space

Sample 2: Term plan

Week	Student tasks	Required resources	Assessment procedures
1–3			
4–6			
7–10			

Sample 3: Lesson plan

<table>
<tr><td>Teaching group
Individual
Whole class
Team group ✓</td><td>Required materials</td></tr>
<tr><td>Learning strategies
Collaborating
Interpreting
Predicting ✓
Investigating
Recording ✓
Justifying
Changing
Communicating</td><td>Specific content—lesson plan</td></tr>
<tr><td>Learning outcomes</td><td>Assessment tasks</td></tr>
<tr><td>Related outcomes from other subjects</td><td>Integrated activities</td></tr>
</table>

Assessment templates

Defining terms

Assessment refers to the collection and analysis of data about student behaviour and progress. Assessment data can also be used to make program decisions.

Evaluation refers to the process of using assessment information to make judgments about the effectiveness of teaching programs and to improve teaching practice so as to improve student learning.

Reporting refers to the procedures where assessment information is communicated to others (usually parents, students and other teachers) to inform and assist student learning.

Record-keeping is the documentation we keep when we assess and evaluate. Assessment information needs to be recorded in ways which enable the teacher to construct a profile of learning for each student.

An **Outcome** can be defined as a behaviour that students will demonstrate after learning experiences. Outcomes generally relate to knowledge and skills. Outcomes are usually broad and relate to long-term learning. Outcomes are demonstrable, sequential and observable.

Assessment templates

The following templates are designed to give teachers suggestions on recording assessment information. They are not meant to be prescriptive, but to assist teachers in designing their own assessment records.

Sample 1: Skills assessment template

Science—skills checklist

Name: ______________________ **Date:** ______________

Topic	Skills	Achieved ✓			Comments
		Most of the time	Some of the time	Rarely	
Working scientifically	**Investigating** • Collect information • Explore phenomena • Seek reasons for happenings • Make a hypothesis • Look for patterns and meanings • Measure accurately • Access resources • Design experiments • Think carefully about problems • Make plans • Handle materials and equipment • Carry out investigations • Represent information • Use references • Cooperate with others • Clarify and challenge values • Express a point of view • Listen actively • Formulate questions • Perform an experiment • Work safely **Comprehending** • Make decisions • Solve problems • Make predictions • Take actions • Classify using characteristics • Make oral and written reports • Think logically • Analyse and interpret information • Make suggestions • Use ideas, theories and principles • Construct meanings • Formulate and elaborate ideas • Make generalisations • Look for alternatives • Make comparisons • Make links • Apply ideas and concepts • Make judgments • Reflect • Draw conclusions • Examine and evaluate				

Topic	Skills	Achieved ✓			Comments
		Most of the time	Some of the time	Rarely	
	Communicating • Interpret information • Observe accurately • Create something new • Compare qualities of different things • Make models • Clarify ideas and concepts • Discuss with others • Listen and question • Respond and debate • Use scientific terminology • Negotiate with others • Support ideas • Argue a position • Construct models • Create presentations • Create tables and graphs • Summarise and report • Write and use scientific reports				
Living things	(Insert your own list of skills here)				
Science in the home	(Insert your own list of skills here)				
Earth and beyond	(Insert your own list of skills here)				

Sample 2: Cognitive skills template

Learning skills assessment checklist

For assessing learning skills, group communication skills and attitudes

Name: ______________________________ **Date:** ________________

Skills	Skills observed ✓	Comments
Learning skills • can form and ask questions • can follow instructions • can find information • can find required information • can express ideas clearly and correctly • can critically reflect on own work • can organise self efficiently • understands how to improve own work • manages use of time well		
Group skills • follows group rules • works cooperatively within a team • contributes to discussions without dominating • listens while other people speak • accommodates different points of view		
Attitudes • respects other students' point of view • participates freely in activities • works in a constructive and positive way • values the beliefs held by other students		

Sample 3: Student self-assessment template

Student self-assessment checklist

Name: ______________________________ **Date:** ______________

Skills	Can do ✓
My learning skills • I can ask questions • I can follow instructions • I can find the information that I need • I can express myself clearly and correctly • I can think about what was right and wrong about my work • I can work neatly • I am well organised • I understand how to improve my work • I use my time well	
My group skills • I can work well with others in a group • I can listen when others are talking • I can discuss something without getting angry	
My attitudes • I can listen and respect what others have to say • I can take responsibility for my own work • I can share in a group activity • I can learn from my mistakes	
My comments	

Sample 4: Group assessment template

Group assessment template

Date: ______________________

Names of group members:

____

____

Name of group: ______________________
Activity:

____

____

____

What things did your group do really well?

____

____

____

What things does your group need to improve?

____

____

____

What are you going to do to change the way your group works?

____

____

____

Sample 5: Term self-assessment template

My term report

Name: ____________________

I rate my working habits this term as:

I am a quiet worker	/10
I am a neat worker	/10
I finish my work on time	/10
I am able to work by myself	/10
I work well in groups	/10

What I did well this term

What I plan to improve on next term

What I would like to see changed next term

What I really liked doing this term

What I didn't like doing this term

Glossary

acids	a family of substances that contain the element hydrogen and have a sour taste; strong acids can be very corrosive
algae	simple green plants that usually live in water or damp places e.g. seaweed
alkali	a base that is soluble in water
alloy	a metal made by mixing two or more different metals
alluvial gold	small pieces of gold carried by rivers where it settles on the bottom
amphibian	an animal that is able to live on land and in water by breathing through the skin and lungs e.g. frog
andesite	a kind of igneous rock
anther	the structure from which pollen is released
armature	a rotating electromagnet in an electric motor
asexual reproduction	a type of reproduction in which a new individual is produced from one parent
atmosphere	the layer of gases that surrounds the Earth
atmospheric pressure	the weight of air pushing down on the Earth
axis	an imaginary line through the centre of the Earth; the line on the left-hand side or bottom of a graph
basalt	a kind of igneous rock
bases	a family of substances that react with acids; strong bases can be very corrosive
binary fission	the process where one cell divides into two cells and the contents of the two cells are shared
biodegradable	materials that can rot or be broken down by decay due to small living things like bacteria and fungi
block and tackle	a block of pulleys together with the rope or chain
brass	an alloy made from copper and zinc
brittle	hard but breaks easily
bronze	an alloy made from copper and tin
budding	asexual reproduction by forming a bud that slowly develops into a new individual
burr	hooks on the coat of a seed that help them to stick to the fur of animals
calibration	to put marks on an instrument so that it can be used to measure accurately
carpel	the structure that contains the ovary in plants
casting	pouring liquid metal or plastic into a mould to make an object with a particular shape
Celsius	a scale from 0 to 100 used to measure temperature
chemical properties	the characteristics of a material and how it reacts with other substances
circuit	a path around which electricity can flow that is usually made of wires
clearfelling	cutting down all the trees in the forest
cocoon	a special case that many insects spin at the end of the larval stage
communication	the process in which a message is sent, transmitted and received
commutator	part of an electric motor that reverses the direction of the current in the armature so that the armature continues to rotate in one direction

conductor	something that lets heat or electricity pass through easily
conduction	the way in which heat moves in a solid
conserve	to use materials carefully so that they will last as long as possible
contraction	the decrease in size that occurs when some substances are cooled
control	the part of an experiment in which no changes are made so that the result can be compared with the test; *see also* test
convection	the movement of heat that occurs when hot air expands and floats upwards and cooler air moves in to take its place
corrosion	a process that changes and spoils metals e.g. rusting
corrosive	something that can cause serious burns to the skin and also make holes in clothes e.g. strong acids and strong bases
cross-pollination	pollen that is carried from stamens to carpels on another plant of the same type
data	information that has been collected in an investigation
degree	a unit of temperature
density	the heaviness of an object for its size; the amount of material in a given space
dispersal	the scattering or spreading of seeds
drift net	a long net that is allowed to float behind a boat in order to catch fish
durable	materials that do not wear out easily
edible	something that can be eaten
efficiency	the energy that we get out divided by the energy that we put in multiplied by 100%
egg	a female sex cell
electrodes	metal plates that dip into a liquid and are used to pass an electric current through the liquid
electromagnet	the magnetic effect that is created when an electric current flows in a coil
electromagnetic radiation	the way in which heat and light travel from the Sun
embryo	a zygote that has divided and grown
energy	energy is the ability to do work; there are different types of energy
exoskeleton	the outside covering of insects, prawns and crabs
expansion	the increase in size that occurs when some substances are heated
external fertilisation	the joining of a male sex cell and female sex cell outside the body of the female
extrusive rocks	igneous rocks that are formed when magma reaches the surface of the Earth
fair	sensible, reasonable, logical
fern	a green plant that has no flowers but reproduces by producing spores on the underside of the fronds
fertilisation	the joining of a male sex cell with a female sex cell
filament	a wire with high resistance
fissure	a deep crack
flammable	materials that burn easily
flexible	may be bent easily
flowering plant	a plant that has enclosed seeds formed within a fruit that develops from a flower

foetus	the developing baby from the third month of development until birth in humans
force	a push or a pull that usually makes something move or change direction
fossil	the remains of plants or animals that lived thousands of years ago
frogspawn	frog eggs that have been laid in water
fruit	a complete ovary after fertilisation
fulcrum	a fixed point or pivot that is used to make a lever work
fungi	plants that have no chlorophyll but live on the dead remains of other plants and animals
gas	matter that has no fixed volume and no fixed shape
geostationary satellite	a satellite that appears to be stationary above one place on the Earth's equator
granite	a kind of igneous rock
gravity	the force that pulls objects down
hard	difficult to scratch and not easy to wear away
heavenly bodies	the Sun, Moon, planets and stars
horizontal	parallel to the bottom of the page or horizon
hornfels	a common type of metamorphic rock
hydro-electricity	electricity made by generators driven by running water
igneous rock	rock formed from magma that has cooled and solidified at the Earth's surface (volcanic rock) or deep within the Earth's surface (plutonic rock)
imago	the adult stage of complete metamorphosis in the life cycle of an insect
inclined plane	a slope, such as a ramp, that allows heavy objects to be lifted or raised by smaller forces
indicator	a dye that will change colour when mixed with an acid or a base
inedible	something that should not be eaten
insulator	something that stops heat or electricity passing through
internal fertilisation	the joining of a male sex cell and female sex cell inside the body of the female
intrusive rocks	igneous rocks that are formed inside the Earth
joule (J)	a unit of work
kilojoule (kJ)	a unit of energy, equal to 1000 joules; the symbol for kilojoule is kJ
kinetic energy	moving energy
larva	a young insect
life cycle	the different stages a living thing goes through as it grows and develops from an egg to a mature adult
liquid	matter that has a fixed volume but no fixed shape
litmus	a common indicator
magma	molten rock inside the earth
marble	a metamorphic rock that is made from the sedimentary rock limestone
mass	the quantity of substance or amount of material in something
matter	any material or substance that has mass and takes up space
mechanical advantage	a force ratio which we calculate by dividing the load by the effort
megajoule (mJ)	a million joules
metal	solids that are usually hard and can be flattened into sheets and stretched into wires

metamorphic rock	rock that has been changed because of high temperature and pressure; it is harder and looks different
metamorphosis	a process of change e.g. the separate stages that an insect goes through in its life cycle; during incomplete metamorphosis insects go through three stages: egg, larva or nymph and adult; during complete metamorphosis there are four separate stages: egg, larva, pupa and adult
mineral ores	rocks that contain metals
minerals	the chemical elements and chemical compounds that make up rocks
molten	rock or metal that has been heated to a very high temperature and has become a thick sticky liquid
moss	a simple green land plant that lives in cool, damp places
mould	a shape or hole which is left by the body of an animal in mud, clay or ash; when the hole is filled it becomes a cast which has the same shape as the original animal
natural materials	materials that come from plants, animals and the Earth
neutralisation	the type of reaction that occurs when an acid mixes with a base to form a neutral solution
non-biodegradable	materials that do not rot or decay
non-renewable	something that cannot easily be replaced
nymph	a young insect that looks very much like the adult
obsidian	a hard, shiny black igneous rock that can be used to make sharp tools
ore	the rocks from which we obtain metals
ore body	a large amount of ore
overfishing	catching more fish than are born and grow to maturity
ovule	a female sex cell or egg in plants
panning	a way of obtaining gold by putting sand, gravel and water in a metal pan and moving it round in a circle
parallel circuit	a circuit made from several loops in which the current divides and flows to each part separately
pasteurisation	killing germs that cause food to become rotten by heating to 55°C
penis	male reproductive organ in mammals that leaves the sperm inside the body of the female so that fertilisation can occur
pH scale	a scale of numbers from 0 to 14 that is used to measure the strength of an acid or base
physical properties	the characteristics of a material and how it behaves
pivot	*see* fulcrum
placenta	the structure that attaches the embryo to the uterus and which passes food and oxygen from the mother to the embryo and carries waste from the embryo to the mother
placer deposit	the place where alluvial gold is found
pollen	male sex cells in plants
pollination	the movement of pollen from one flower to another flower
pollution	materials that end up in rivers, the sea, on the land or in the air that can spoil the environment and harm living things

porous will allow water to pass through

processed materials materials that people have made or manufactured e.g. flour and cement

pulley a simple machine that consists of a rope, chain or belt stretched over the rim of a wheel

pupa third stage of complete metamorphosis in the life cycle of insects that does not feed at all

quarantine special rules to make sure that plant and animal pests and diseases are not carried from country to country

radiation the way in which light and heat travel through air

raw materials naturally occurring materials that are used to make products

recycling using materials again instead of being thrown away; a way of conserving materials

regeneration asexual reproduction in which a new individual develops from pieces of the adult

renewable something that can be replaced

resource something that can be used to meet the needs of people

royalties money that is paid to landowners where timber or minerals are removed

satellite something that orbits or travels around the Sun, the Earth or another planet

seed a fertilised cell that has grown by cell division in the ovary; each seed contains an embryo, a food store and a thick coat for protection

self-pollination pollen that is carried from stamens to carpels on the same plant

series circuit a simple circuit in which everything is connected in a line or single loop

sexual reproduction a type of reproduction in which a new individual is produced from two parents

sediment small particles of solid that settle at the bottom of a liquid

sedimentary rock rock that is formed from sediments that have been squashed or compressed

selective logging cutting down only certain types and sizes of trees

simple fission *see* binary fission

solar from the Sun

solar system the Sun and the family of eight planets, moons and asteroids

solid matter that has a fixed volume and a fixed shape

space the empty place that surrounds or lies between the stars and planets

space probe a spacecraft that flies by or lands on the surface of a heavenly body in the solar system

space shuttle a space craft that takes off like a rocket, orbits the Earth and lands like an aeroplane

space station a satellite that is big enough for people to live in

spawning laying eggs in water e.g. fish and some frogs

sperm male sex cells in animals

spontaneous generation the idea or theory that living things just seemed to appear by themselves

spores single cells that are very light and usually produced in large numbers during asexual reproduction

stamen the structure that hold the grains of pollen that contain the male sex cells

state the condition of matter—whether it is a solid, liquid or gas

stem	part of the shoot of a flowering plant that supports the leaves, buds, flowers and fruits
stock	the animals or plants that are kept or left so that they will reproduce
synthetic materials	processed materials that are made from chemicals or artificial substances
tadpole	the embryo of a frog that develops from a fertilised egg
tailings	the waste from ore that mining companies produce
telescope	an instrument that is used to look at heavenly bodies
temperature	a measure of how hot something is
terminals	the parts of a battery to which the wires are connected
test	the part of an experiment in which changes are made so that the result can be compared with the control; *see also* control
testes	the place where sperm cells are produced in vertebrates
thermometer	the instrument used to measure temperature
thermostat	a switch that uses temperature to turn on and off
translucent	lets light through but scatters it; opaque or obscure
transparent	lets light through or 'see-through'
trawling	catching fish or prawns by dragging a large net behind a boat
treated timber	wood that has been soaked or sprayed with a chemical solution to help stop it rotting or being eaten by insects
umbilical cord	the tube that joins the embryo to the placenta
uterus	the organ inside the body of a female placental mammal in which the embryo develops; also called the womb
vacuum flask	a bottle with a double wall that is used to keep food and drinks hot or cold
vagina	female reproductive organ in mammals that the penis enters and through which the baby passes when it is born
vegetative reproduction	asexual reproduction in plants that occurs when a new individual is produced from any part except the flower
vertical	at right angles to the bottom of the page or the horizon
waterproof	will not allow water to pass through
weight	the downward pull of the Earth's gravity on the mass of an object
zygote	the single cell that is formed as a result of fertilisation

Teacher notes

Teacher notes

Teacher notes

Teacher notes